The Story of Job

JESSIE PENN-LEWIS

RARE CHRISTIAN BOOKS
19275 Highway 28
Dixon, MO 65459
Ph./Fax: (573) 336-7316

The Story of Job

JESSIE PENN-LEWIS

CHRISTIAN · LITERATURE · CRUSADE
Fort Washington, Pennsylvania 19034

CHRISTIAN LITERATURE CRUSADE

U.S.A.
P.O. Box 1449, Fort Washington, PA 19034

GREAT BRITAIN
51 The Dean, Alresford, Hants., SO24 9BJ

AUSTRALIA
P.O. Box 91, Pennant Hills, N.S.W. 2120

NEW ZEALAND
10 MacArthur Street, Feilding

Originally published in England by
THE OVERCOMER LITERATURE TRUST, LTD.

First American edition 1996
This printing 1996

Cover photo: SuperStock

ISBN 0-87508-736-1

PRINTED IN THE UNITED STATES OF AMERICA

EDITOR'S NOTE

Though written over ninety years ago, and requiring some updating of the language to speak clearly to today's readers, the truths of this devotional exposition of Job are as pertinent now as ever.

Mrs. Penn-Lewis was granted by God a special enduement of power for service, and her spoken ministry was greatly effective. Today, years later, her messages in print are still fresh and vital, and are being used to bring help and blessing to many all over the world. It is recorded that on one occasion a gentleman with a strong prejudice against the ministry of women heard her speak at a conference, and said to her afterwards: "I would not have believed it possible, had I not seen it, that God would use *a woman* like that." "God never does use a woman like that," was her quick response, "or *a man* either! God only uses the *new creation*."

PREFACE

THE Book of Job has been a treasure-store to me ever since I went through it with my Bible class in 1895. However, many deeper lessons of the past seven years have been necessary before I could be entrusted by the Lord with the privilege of drawing forth from it, in even a small measure, the message it particularly contains for the people of God in these turbulent days.

As we look out upon the world we see the true gold of God's elect in the furnace of trial on every hand. If not in trials of "mockings and scourgings . . . of bonds and imprisonments," yet are they individually in some furnace "made exceeding hot," and many, it may be, are tried in some measure after the pattern of the Lord's dealing with Job.

This treatise on the experiences of Job I send forth in the Master's name to all the children of God who are walking with Him in integrity of heart and loyal obedience to His known will but who are placed by Him in such a fiery trial that they are often perplexed and dismayed.

May the Eternal Spirit graciously use this message to give light upon the ways of God and to minister to them the comfort of God while in the crucible.

As regards the scope of this book, a little explanation is necessary.

I have not attempted a minute exegesis of the text of Scripture. Others with far more resources in scholarship and time have been given this service. But I have sought rather to give a rapid outline of the story of Job from the *experiential standpoint,* and in narrative form so as to present it in simplicity to the hearts of those for whom it may have been sent by God. In the Appendix I have added a few brief extracts from the writings of others which seem to be appropriate.

I have also avoided all reference to controversial questions, scholastic and spiritual, so that the Word of God might convey its own message as the Divine Spirit may be pleased to apply it to the needs of the children of God.

In conclusion, I earnestly ask all who read this book to take for themselves only the portion that commends itself to them as *from the Spirit of God for their own heart's need* and to leave the remainder for His use to those other souls for whom it may have been given.

I have used the 1881 Revised Version of the Bible with the exception of some alternative readings from the Authorized Version.

Jessie Penn-Lewis
June, 1902

CONTENTS

INTRODUCTION

"By faith Abel offered unto God a . . . sacrifice . . . through which he had witness borne to him that he was righteous." (Heb. 11:4)

THE MAN NAMED JOB

"There was a man in the land of Uz whose name was Job." (Job 1:1)

THE spirit of the present age unconsciously affects even those who acknowledge that "every Scripture is inspired of God and profitable for teaching, for reproof, for correction, for discipline which is in righteousness."

"Was Job a real person?" is the question that springs to the lips of some as soon as his name is mentioned.

The Omniscient Lord foresaw these perilous times and happily provided in later scriptures the answer to this question.

The prophet Ezekiel expressly records that the word of the Lord came to him saying, "Son of man, when a land sinneth against Me, . . . though these three men, Noah, Daniel, and *Job* were in it, they should but deliver their own souls by their righteousness" (Ezekiel 14:13–14, 20).

We may rest assured that the God of Truth would not have classed Job with Noah and Daniel as one of *three righteous men* had he been but a mythical personage and the Book of Job nought else but a literary masterpiece.

11

The Apostle James also speaks of Job and appears to include him among "the prophets who spake in the name of the Lord" who were examples of "suffering and of patience" (James 5:10). He is among the "blessed" ones who endured. "*Ye have heard*," he writes, "*of the endurance of Job,* and have seen [in his case] the *end of the Lord,* how that the Lord is full of pity, and merciful" (James 5:11, mg.).

It is very evident that the early Christians knew the reality of Job's history and regarded him as an example of patience and his life story as an encouragement to trust in the compassion and love of God.

The Jews have tenaciously kept the Book of Job in their canon of Scripture. It is said to be the oldest book extant and to have been written some two thousand years before Christ.

It is impossible to speak with absolute certainty upon these two last points, but on general internal evidence some scholars assign the book to the period of the time of Abraham. "That it is inspired appears from the fact that the Apostle Paul quotes it (Job 5:13, in 1 Cor. 3:19) with the formula *It is written.* Our Saviour also (Matt. 24:28) plainly refers to Job 39:30" (Fausset).

The Seventy in their translation say that Job lived some two hundred and forty years, one hundred and forty being after his affliction. It is therefore quite possible, as some think, that he knew and often talked with Shem the son of Noah, and that Job himself may have been one of the line of sacred prophets spoken of by Zachariah under the inspiration of the Holy Spirit as having been God's spokesmen "since the world began" (Luke 1:70).

In the sacred record Job is described as the "greatest of all the children of the East." Most scholars are agreed that he was of princely rank, some even maintaining that he was a real king. His possessions were

very great and consisted of thousands of sheep and
camels, many hundred yoke of oxen and she-asses,
and "a very great household."

Seven sons and three daughters, with his wife,
formed his immediate family circle; and at the time of
the opening of the Scripture story the sons appear
to each have had their own households, doubtless
maintained in conformity with their father's wealth
and dignity.

It is also evident that Job was cultured and learned
to an advanced degree, for in his book we find "a
familiarity with writing, engraving in stone, mining,
metallurgy, building, shipping, natural history, as-
tronomy, and science in general" (Seiss).

Above all we are left in no doubt as to Job's personal character. The very first words of the book are
given to describing this, while it is silent as to much
that is mere detail in his history.

Again and again we find this method in both the
Old and New Testaments. The sacred writings are not
intended to satisfy our curiosity. They describe lives
and histories only so far as to fulfill the main purpose of God in winning men back to Himself.

It is thus in the case of Job. A very few words
suffice to tell us of his position, wealth, and family
circle, and then we are at once introduced to a series
of events in his life of momentous import and teaching for all the people of God long after Job himself
has passed away.

Job's portrait as a man of God is sketched for us in
a few brief words:

". . . that man was perfect and upright, and one that
feared God, and eschewed evil" (Job 1:1).

It is of the greatest importance that we should fully
recognize Job's spiritual character at the time when
he was placed in the furnace of trial. He is described
as "perfect and upright," and Jehovah uses the very

same language when speaking of him in the council
of heaven.

Job's subsequent history interprets this description and makes it clear that he was called a "perfect"
man simply in the sense of being whole-hearted and
sincere in his loyalty to God. He was not of double
heart ("a heart and a heart" as in the expressive
marginal reading of 1 Chronicles 12:33), seeking to
serve two masters, God and himself. This whole-
hearted loyalty to God made him upright in his life
before men. He feared God and shunned evil.

The "fear of the Lord" is the Old Testament expression descriptive of the "understanding" mentioned by
the Apostle John when he wrote to the "little children" who "knew the Father," saying, He *hath given
us an understanding,* that we *know* Him that is true"
(1 John 5:20).

This "fear of the Lord" or "understanding" is a
divine sensitiveness to His will, an intuitive knowledge of it springing out of a close fellowship with God
Himself. Job had this fear of God in a marked degree,
and as a consequence he abstained from everything
evil (Septuagint).

The extent of our knowledge of God, our "quick
understanding" of His mind and will, carries with it a
proportionate knowledge of the exceeding sinfulness
of sin. Just so far as we truly know God shall we have
a godly awe of Him and dread to grieve Him.

Job's "fear of the Lord" and a sensitiveness to sin
we see carried out in practice, not only in the shunning of evil so far as he knew a thing to be evil but in
his instinctive consciousness of the need of sacrifice,
or the shedding of blood, for the remission of even
sins of ignorance. He anticipated the law given afterwards to Israel: "And if anyone sin . . . though he
knew it not, *yet is he guilty*" (Leviticus 5:17).

Taught by God, he anticipated the "better sacrifice" referred to in Hebrews 9:23, and the "blood of sprinkling" speaking evermore within the veil for the continual cleansing of all who walk in fellowship with God (1 John 1:7).

Job knew the Lord in His holiness, and in his fear of sinning against Him he rose early in the morning to offer sacrifice to God on behalf of his children, lest in their days of feasting they might have failed in the recollection of Jehovah's presence, gone beyond the limit of restraint in any degree, had a thought of evil in their minds (Septuagint), or blasphemed God in their hearts (Job 1:5, margin).

What a glimpse we have here into Job's knowledge of God. He understood that remission was needed, *through a sacrifice,* even for a momentary forgetfulness of the presence of God.

His offering of the burnt offerings "continually" (that is, as his regular custom) also shows that his fear of God was not spasmodic or occasional, when under some great pressure, but that it was a deeply rooted principle of his life governing all his actions. In short, his one and only aim was to be true to God, upright in life, and clear of all that was sin, so far as he knew anything to be sin, and of all that might be evil in the sight of God both for himself and his family.

Further features of Job's godly character and life we shall see brought out more fully as we trace his story. The portrait will be filled out in more detail; but the Divine Spirit, who inspired the record, emphasizes the secret of his life at the very commencement of the history of his sufferings.

Job's fear of God and walk of integrity before Him must be clearly recognized if we are to understand the meaning of his trial.

CHAPTER 1

"To the intent that now unto the principalities and the powers in the heavenly places might be made known through the church the manifold wisdom of God." (Ephesians 3:10)

A SCENE IN HEAVEN, AND THE ADVERSARY'S CHALLENGE

"Now there was a day when the sons of God came to present themselves before the Lord, and Satan [*"the Adversary,"* mg.] came also among them." (Job 1:6)

AFTER a brief description of Job's personal character, his wealth, position and family, we have opened suddenly before us a scene in heaven. The veil is drawn aside, and we are shown Jehovah seated upon His throne in the midst of His council of holy ones.

It is an audience day in the court of the King of kings. The "sons of God," or angels, present themselves before the Lord to report upon their various duties.

Satan, the "Adversary," enters among them in his capacity as "prince of this world" and "prince of the power of the air." "He that is called the Devil and Satan, the deceiver of the whole inhabited earth, . . . the accuser of our brethren" (Revelation 12:9–10, mg.).

Passages from other parts of the Scriptures confirm, almost in detail, this description of the Lord of Hosts in council assembled.

David speaks of the "assembly of the holy ones"

17

and asks, "Who among the sons of the mighty is like unto the Lord, a God very terrible in the council of the holy ones?" (Psalm 89:5–7).

Daniel sees and hears the "holy ones" speaking one to the other of the purposes of God on the earth, and the sentence upon Nebuchadnezzar was apparently decreed by the whole council of God assembled and a "holy one" entrusted with its fulfillment.

Zechariah sees Joshua the high priest standing before the Lord and tells how those that "stood by" were bidden to remove the filthy garments and clothe him with a change of raiment (Zechariah 3:4).

We may clearly gather, too, that there are degrees of authority in this heavenly assembly of the "sons of the Mighty," for we read of two *archangels*, Gabriel and Michael, and of "*seven presence angels*," besides all the holy ones or "*watchers*" spoken of by Daniel.

Godet says that the meaning of Gabriel's name is "*God's hero*," and that he is the "active executor of God's designs for the salvation of men." He was the chosen messenger sent to Mary to foretell the birth of her Saviour and Son.

The name of the archangel Michael means "*Who is like unto God?*" and his work is to "overthrow every thing that dares to make itself equal with God," while Gabriel "hastens the realization of His plans."*

Gabriel was sent to make Daniel skillful in understanding the things of God (9:21–22), while Michael, "one of the chief princes," came to the help of the Divine Man in His conflict with the opposing forces of darkness while on His way to His interview with Daniel (10:13).

Again Michael is spoken of as the "great prince" especially entrusted with the interests of the people of God (Daniel 12:1), and the character of his work is

---

* Godet, *Biblical Studies*, p. 15

referred to also in the letter of the Apostle Jude, where he speaks of Michael as contending with the devil for the body of Moses.

The veil is drawn aside once more in the Book of Revelation, and we see Michael leading forth the hosts of the Lord against the hosts of darkness in that great and terrible war in heaven, when the rebel prince of the power of the air is finally cast out of the heavenly places and cast down to the earth, and all his angels with him (12:7–9).

These are some of the passages in the Scriptures giving glimpses into the court of heaven. We shall not take time to mention others that speak of the high calling of God in Christ Jesus for us who were once far off and dead in trespasses and sins. The *angels*, after all, are but "ministering spirits" sent forth to do service to them who shall be heirs of salvation; for we, the redeemed among men, are called not only to *stand before* the throne but to be *joint-heirs* with Him who has sat down upon His Father's throne.

The character of Satan as the adversary and accuser, so vividly portrayed in the story of Job, is also abundantly verified in other passages of Scripture, and we cannot question but that the veil is really drawn aside for a brief glimpse into the spiritual world.

The Adversary

> "The Lord said unto Satan, Whence comest thou? . . . [He] said, From going to and fro in the earth, and from walking up and down in it." (Job 1:7)

Satan apparently had the official right to enter the presence of Jehovah on an "audience day." He is the rebel prince of the earth, the "spirit that now worketh in the sons of disobedience"; the "god of this age" who blinds the thoughts of the unbelieving; the leader of the principalities and powers of "the world-rulers of this darkness," the spiritual hosts of wickedness in the heavenly places.

A promise had been given before the time of Job that the "Seed" who would bruise Satan's head, destroy his works and bring him to nought, would come in the fullness of time; but as yet the rebel prince was not deprived of his realm. He boldly enters the presence of Jehovah among the other servants of the King. To the question "Whence comest thou?" he replies that he has come "from going to and fro in the earth, and from walking up and down in it."

"Going to and fro" and *"walking up and down"*—so the adversary describes his occupation. The picture given is that he has been roaming around in the "heat of haste." He has been hurrying through the inhabited earth "as a roaring lion seeking whom he may devour" or as an "unclean spirit seeking rest" and finding none.

This fallen archangel imparts his feverish spirit to those who are yet under his control, for "the wicked are like the troubled sea; for it cannot rest. . . . There is no peace, saith my God, to the wicked" (Isaiah 57:20–21).

We should pay special heed to this self-given description of the Adversary's character and note the contrast between his feverish "heat of haste" and the calm walk of the Son of God in His life on earth.

The devil rushes to and fro with restless energy through the realms he has betrayed, causing tumult and unrest wherever he goes. The Son of God walked in calm peace through the world He came to save, and rest and blessing and life were given by Him on every hand.

No feverish heat of haste ever comes from God; and just as far as the soul becomes a "partaker of the Divine nature" will it partake of the calm, restful power so strikingly manifested in the Man Christ Jesus.

Let us contrast, too, the difference between the movements of Gabriel—moving only to fulfill the will of God and in obedience to the commands of God— and this restless fallen archangel. Removed from his place in the order of God, Satan is a wandering star, aimless and dissatisfied, with no joy in heaven or earth except in tempting others and bringing them into the same sore plight as himself.

The Question of Jehovah

> "The Lord said unto Satan, Hast thou considered My servant Job? for there is none like him in the earth. . . ." (Job 1:8)

The Lord well knew what the adversary's feverish hurry to and fro in the earth meant! It boded no good to any soul, much less to faithful servants of God.

"Hast thou *set thy heart* [mg.] on My servant Job?" asks Jehovah. "There is none like him in the earth, a man *blameless, true, godly, abstaining from everything evil*" (Septuagint).

What a testimony to Job before all the council of heaven!

"None like him in the earth!" Does this not mean that he was the ripest, most matured and choicest servant of God among all who in his day sought to serve Jehovah in integrity of heart and life? And does it not imply that he was the one most fitted to be entrusted with the service of suffering, being chosen as *a pattern of the ways of God* in the ages to come for all His children in the furnace of trial?

Paul the Apostle understood this privilege of being chosen by God as an object lesson to others regarding the dealings of God. "I obtained mercy," he writes, "that *in me first* Jesus Christ might show forth all longsuffering, for a pattern" (1 Timothy 1:16, A.V.).

Even so was Job chosen by God to be an example of His compassion and tender mercy in placing His loved ones in the crucible—that their affliction, which is but for a moment, might work for them an "exceeding weight of glory."

There was "none like him in the earth" also to the prince of darkness. Job was "a city set on a hill that [could not] be hid." Of all men, he could not live or die unto himself; his fall would result in the casting down of many. An obvious target for the devil he surely must be, one upon whom Satan's heart would be set with unceasing thought and fiendish plans for his undoing.

The Adversary's reply to the Lord's question shows that he *had* considered Job to some purpose. He was prepared with his answer as he quickly says, *"Doth Job fear God for nought?"*

True to his character, he sneeringly casts a doubt upon the integrity of Job's motives in thus being "blameless, true, godly, and abstaining from everything evil." He suggests that Job fears God for *all that he gets from Him* and not purely for His glory.

Just in the same way did the serpent suggest to Eve that God was grudging to His creatures in withholding from them the fruit of the tree of knowledge, and in just the same way today does he whisper to his subjects that selfish motives surely must lie at the back of all service to God. Disinterested love and service on the part of God or man is beyond the imagination of the devil and of those who are in his power.

Satan goes on to prove to Jehovah that his insinuation is borne out by facts, as he adds, "Hast not Thou *made an hedge* about him, and about his house, and about all that he hath, on every side?" The devil knew well this "hedge" of God's protecting

care, for he had met the divine environment on whichever side he had sought to attack the servant of God.

What a word of cheer to every faithful heart! The
"hedge" is not only around the praying one but *about
his house* and about all that he has on every side!

Moreover, Satan complains that God had not only
"set an hedge" about Job and protected him, but He
had *"blessed the work of his hands"* and increased
his substance in the land (Job 1:10). What opportunity was there for Job to prove that his integrity and
loyalty to God were disinterested and true? *Jehovah*
might see his heart and know that he was loyal at the
core, but *who else* could believe this when they saw
him with nothing but prosperity and blessing on
every side?

The Adversary's Challenge

> "Put forth Thine hand now, and touch all that he
> hath, and he will renounce Thee to Thy face." (Job
> 1:11)

Was this challenge the *object* that the fallen archangel had in his mind when he entered the audience
chamber of the King on that occasion?

The Adversary had "set his heart" upon Job. He
had walked around that "hedge"; and so long as Job
had kept within the circle of the presence round
about him, he had found no way of reaching him. If
Satan could but get that "hedge" removed, he thought
he could make this so-called "godly man" as bitterly
rebellious against the Lord as he was himself.

This rebel archangel had once sought to exalt his
throne above the "stars of God." He had dared to say,
"I will be like the Most High," but through his pre-
sumption he had been cast down to hell. If he who
had once been "perfect in beauty," a daystar and son

of the morning, had fallen from his high estate and become the arch-enemy of God, there was hope then that this son of Adam, a member of a fallen race, would be brought down with him. That Job should walk with God in loyal trust and obedience was more than Satan could endure.

Boldly he challenges the integrity of Job in the full assembly of the council of heaven around their King, saying to Jehovah: "Thou *sayest* that Thy servant is upright and true to Thee; *prove it* by touching all that he hath. If Thou doest take away all that Thou hast given him, he will cease to serve Thee; he will renounce his allegiance not in secret, *but to Thy face.*"

What else could Jehovah do but accept the challenge and allow His servant to be put to the test? The council members of heaven have listened to the debate and have heard Jehovah's estimate of His godly servant and the insinuating sneer of the fallen angel as to his integrity. This daring accusation cannot be overlooked. *The word of Jehovah is in question.* The loyalty of Job shall be proved. All heaven shall know that Jehovah can be loved and worshiped for *Himself,* even by a son of Adam.

With joy the adversary sees the challenge accepted. The "hedge" of the Lord's protection around Job is removed by the words, "Behold, all that he hath is in thy power; only upon *himself* put not forth thine hand" (Job 1:12).

"*So Satan went forth. . . .*"

The Adversary's Devices

"It fell on a day. . . ." (Job 1:13–19)

In brief and vivid language we now have described the Adversary's attacks upon the possessions of Job. His plan had been carefully thought out with all the skill that had been gained since he tempted Eve in Eden.

Job must be taken unawares, and under the pressure of sudden loss forced to an impulsive renunciation of God. The devil well knew Job would not do it coolly and deliberately.

The character of a man is generally revealed in the hour of sudden crisis. With no time for recollection, what is in the heart will suddenly break out—especially under the pressure of great anguish and pain.

Times of joyous festivity, too, are times when men are not so likely to be on guard, and "bad news" in the midst of mirth is always more appalling.

The subtle Adversary chooses the time carefully. On a day of festivity among the sons and daughters of Job, a messenger comes to him to tell him that the "Sabeans" have suddenly fallen upon his cattle in the field, taken them away, and slain all the servants with none but the messenger left!

Before the man has finished speaking, another arrives with the news that fire from heaven has fallen and burned up Job's sheep and their shepherds, with only the messenger himself having escaped to tell him! Immediately a third arrives to say that other bands of robbers have carried away the camels and slain those servants with the sword, save only the one particular person spared to carry the news.

All this means utter *ruin* as far as earthly substance is concerned! The coincidence of each thing happening so closely together, and each group of servants being slain with only the *one* escaped to tell the tale might well have suggested to Job that more than natural causes lay behind these sudden blows, for the soul that walks with God learns to understand and recognize the supernatural powers that lie behind the surface of things in daily life.

But this touching of Job's worldly goods was not

enough. His *real* treasure was in heaven, and "a man's *life* consisteth not in the abundance of the things which he possesseth."

So there is yet more! The devil had reserved his keenest blow to the last. Job has hardly had time to realize that all his wealth was gone when another messenger arrives to tell him that in the midst of their festivities a strong wind had struck the house in which his children were and buried them and the attendants in its ruins. *"They are dead,"* said the servant who carried the news, and again, *"I only am escaped alone to tell thee."* There is no softening of the sorrowful story! *"They are dead"* is blurted out. This is the greatest blow of all, and upon its effect the subtle foe has counted.

Children swept away into eternity in the midst of their festivities! No time to say farewell, no last prayer, no last message—

"Then Job arose, . . . fell down upon the ground, and *worshipped*; and he said, *Naked came I out of my mother's womb,* * and naked shall I return thither: the Lord gave, and the Lord hath taken away; blessed be the name of the Lord"* (Job 1:20–21).

How little Job realized the cloud of witnesses looking on! And what sympathy and joy in His servant's faithfulness there must have been in the heart of God; for in all this adversity *He* had been no adversary, and *He* had not afflicted willingly nor intentionally grieved this man among men!

Job had stood the test. The Adversary was defeated. Instead of rebellion Job had worshiped. The sudden blows had found him standing firm upon God. In one moment his anchored soul had found its refuge. He had "rent his mantle" and "shaved his head," the outward signs of his deep sorrow; but in

---

* Poetically the earth, the universal mother. See Ecclesiastes 12:7—*Fausset.*

his hour of trial his spirit worshiped the God who had blessed him hitherto.

"In all this Job sinned not, nor attributed folly to God" (Job 1:22, mg.). Rather, he *"allowed himself to commit no folly against God"* (Fausset). Job instantly confessed that nothing he possessed was actually his own. It was the *Lord* who had given him wealth; and his children had been laid upon the altar by faith, along with the burnt offerings he had offered to God for them continually. He knew he had *nothing* but that which he had received. Out of dust he had come, and unto dust would he return; he had brought nothing into the world, he could carry nothing out. The Lord had given him everything, and the Lord had the sovereign right to take all things away! Whichever He did, Job would bless the name of the Lord.

CHAPTER 2

"Satan obtained you by asking that he might sift you as wheat, but I have made supplication for thee, that thy faith fail not." (Luke 22:31–32, mg.)

ANOTHER SCENE IN HEAVEN, JOB'S INTEGRITY, AND JOB'S FRIENDS

"Again there was a day when the sons of God came to present themselves before the Lord, and Satan came also. . . ." (Job 2:1)

ONCE more it is an audience day in the court of heaven, and the chief princes and sons of the mighty are gathered in the presence of the King.

The Adversary reappears in their midst, not in any way abashed over his failure to prove his accusation against Job.

Jehovah opens the subject by the formal question to him again, "Whence comest thou?" and Satan returns the same answer as before. The Lord then repeats His description of Job, adding *". . . he still holdeth fast his integrity, although thou movedst Me against him, to destroy him without cause"* (2:3).

Jehovah here declares before His assembled council that all these trials were sent upon Job *"without cause."* His confidence in Job's integrity and faithfulness to Him had been justified. His servant had stood the test. It was fully proved to the accuser that his sneering insinuation as to Job's motives in serving God was without foundation. He was not seeking the "loaves and fishes" after all!

But the Adversary was not silenced. He had a new suggestion ready. All the things that had been taken away did not really touch *Job himself.* His possessions were, after all, only exterior things! True, the children were of his bone and of his flesh; but Job had recognized that they belonged to God even as did all the wealth that He had given him, and so he had surrendered them to Him without hesitation, even though with sorrowing heart.

The Lord had prevented Satan from touching Job himself; therefore the case was not proved, the test had not been sufficient, for so long as a man *himself* is spared he can let other things go. Satan proposes a deeper test. He answers the Lord:

"Skin for skin, yea, all that a man hath will he give for his life. *But put forth Thine hand now, and touch his bone and his flesh, and he will renounce Thee to Thy face*" (2:4–5).

"Just touch Job *himself* and see if he will cling to Thee then! See if in the furnace of suffering he will not renounce his allegiance to Thee. If he has not served Thee for what Thou hast *given* him, at least he serves Thee for what he has *in himself*: the peace of a conscience void of offense, the inward comfort of Thy presence, the reward of integrity in the respect of others," cries the Adversary.

Jehovah again accepts the challenge, and hands over Job to the power of the enemy with but one restriction, "*only spare his life.*"

Let us note here for our comfort that Satan is absolutely under the control of God; he is unable to touch Job, his possessions or his family without the direct permission of Jehovah.

This is confirmed by the words of the Son of God to His disciple Peter. "Simon, behold, Satan *asked to have you* [*obtained you by asking*, mg.], that he might sift you as wheat; but I made supplication for thee, that thy faith fail not" (Luke 22:31–32).

St. Paul also wrote to the Corinthians, *"God is faithful, who will not suffer you to be tempted above that ye are able*; but will with the temptation make also the way of escape, that ye may be able to endure it" (1 Corinthians 10:13).

It is therefore clear that the Adversary must obtain permission before he can touch a servant of God; and that the attack is carefully limited by the all-wise Lord to sifting away the chaff around the true grain of wheat, just as Job was sifted by the direct permission of God.

The Adversary's Attack

"So Satan went forth . . . and smote Job with sore boils from the sole of his foot unto his crown." (Job 2:7)

When Satan does get permission to attack a servant of God, he uses his license to the utmost extent. The limit in Job's case now is his *life*, and a man can live through more than in time of prosperity he thinks he is capable of doing.

The Adversary attacks poor Job's body with a most repulsive, loathsome disease—sore boils from head to foot. He was covered with one universal inflammation. Several well-known diseases endemic to that area of the world produce symptoms like this, so it is impossible to pinpoint it with medical certainty. In any case, the irritation was severe and unending.

Whereupon the stricken Job "took him a potsherd to scrape himself withal; and he sat among the ashes" (2:8).

"In the warm and dry land of the East, the dung is not mixed with straw but is carried in baskets to a place outside the village where it is usually burnt once a month. The rains reduce the ashes to a solid hill of earth, and the place is used for a watchtower, or a place of concourse by the inhabitants of the village.

"There the outcast who has been stricken by some loathsome malady, making him unfit to enter the dwellings of men, lays himself down at night, sheltering himself among the ashes which the sun has warmed" (Wetzstein).

To this ash-mound outside the village the afflicted man repairs, feeling himself an outcast and an object of terror to others by reason of his loathsome condition.

Job, "the greatest of all the children of the East," is compelled to take his place with the beggar and the outcast. His possessions are gone, and he is bereft of his children. He who once had attendants to minister to his every wish must now "take a potsherd to scrape himself"—a piece of a broken earthen vessel, or possibly an instrument made for the purpose, for the sore was too repulsive to touch (Fausset).

Who would recognize the princely Job in that loathsome object sitting among the ashes outside the village where he had once "sat as chief," looked up to as "the most noble of the men of the East" (Septuagint)?

The Integrity of Job

> "Then said his wife unto him, Dost thou still hold fast thine integrity? Renounce God, and die." (Job 2:9)

Job's wife seems to have been the only one left to him, and she appears to have followed him to the ash-mound outside the village. In her anguish over her husband's sufferings, she unknowingly lends her mouth to the Adversary and speaks words similar to those that passed between Jehovah and the Adversary in the council in heaven (2:5).

How did Job's wife know that Job's integrity was in

question? Evidently she had enough spiritual insight to deduce this fact. What she did not realize was that Satan was keenly watching the effect of his attack upon Job and hoped in this critical hour to force him to the point he desired by his wife's words.

In the New Testament we learn from the words of Christ to Peter that the devil can use the lips of our most faithful friends to tempt us in the hour of trial. Peter said to Christ when He spoke of His cross, "Pity Thyself, Lord," but the Son of God at once discerned the source of the words and said unhesitatingly, "Get thee behind Me, *Satan.*"

"*Renounce God and die,*" said Job's loving and faithful wife to her afflicted husband. We do not read of any word she said when she saw their earthly goods swept away, nor of any rebellion over the loss of her children, but now it seems too much to see her husband suffer. It were better for him to be dead than in such a state. The God he had served so loyally must have forsaken him! Is Job still going to persist in "blessing the name of the Lord"? Let him rather "renounce" Him. "Say some word against the Lord" (Septuagint) and die.

"God cannot be a God of love, for He would not let such suffering come to those who serve Him" is often the thought of those who today watch with aching hearts servants of God in severe trial.

But Job again stood the test:

"He said unto her, *Thou speakest as one of the impious women speaketh. What? shall we receive good at the hand of God, and shall we not receive evil?*" (2:10, mg.).

"Only those who do not *know* God speak like this," said Job to his wife. "Such words should not come out of the lips of one who worships Jehovah. It is lawful for Him to do what He *will* with His own. Have we served Him only from selfish interest? Are we

going to cling to Him only in the time of prosperity?
Shall we not accept from His hand *sorrow* and *suffering* as well as joy?"

Job was in reality a thoroughly surrendered soul.
"In all this did not Job sin with his lips" (2:10) because his will was wholly yielded to God, and he was
true, upright, and sincere in his loyalty to Him.

It is, alas, true that many of the children of God, in
one way or another—unconsciously perhaps—serve
Him for the "good" they get in this present world and
in the world to come rather than for Himself alone.

Worldings, too, expect what they call "good" from a
God who is called Love, and misjudge and renounce
Him because of the suffering in the world which they
cannot reconcile with His love. Both Christian and
worldling stumble at the mystery of pain and fail to
understand what a writer has so truly said: "Pain has
other and higher functions than penalty," for "the
outer man must be sacrificed *in the interests of the
man within,* and the world of man without, and unseen worlds beyond" (W. W. Peyton).

Job was a true man of God! Blow upon blow had
come upon him, but his integrity had stood the test.

He proved by his surrender and faith in the faithfulness of God that he had not served Him for all that
He had given him. Whether the Lord gave or the Lord
took away, he still blessed the name of the Lord.

The Friends of Job

> "Now when Job's three friends heard of all this evil
> that was come upon him, they came every one from
> his own place: Eliphaz, . . . Bildad, . . . and Zophar. . . .
> They made an appointment together to come . . . to
> comfort him." (Job 2:11)

Ill news flies apace! The report of Job's troubles
reaches the ears of three of his intimate friends. In

the kindness of their hearts, they agree together to visit him to sympathize with him and comfort him.

The three men make an appointment to journey to the scene of Job's sorrows.

As they go, according to the privilege of intimate friends, they discuss the whole affair from every point of view, and before they see the stricken man they come to their conclusions as to the cause of the "evil" and settle how best to deal with him.

The story of Job bears the impress of reality because it coincides in so many respects with the experiences of people today, for just in the same way that his "friends" discussed Job's plight before they saw him and *settled in their own minds the cause of his troubles,* the friends of afflicted ones act in modern times!

There are few among us who know how to minister the comfort of God. Few are they who know how to *leave their fellows in the hand of God* and encourage them to "*believe* their way through" their paths of trial; and still fewer those who are able to interpret to stricken hearts the *purposes* of God in their afflictions.

Knowing little of the inwardness of things, more often than not we judge by the sight of our eyes and the hearing of our ears and come to conclusions from our own standpoint in proportion to the measure of our own experience.

Eliphaz, Bildad and Zophar approach the village. Afar off they see the ash-mound; but is that Job lying there?

Job, the richest man of the East! Can this pitiable object be the Job that they had known? Alas, alas— they hardly could recognize him and they raised their voices and wept.

How are the mighty fallen!

The three tear their robes in grief and sprinkle dust upon their heads in token of their sorrow.

Having reached the ash-mound, they "sat down with him upon the ground *seven days and seven nights*." This expression aptly describes the fullness of their grief and the long period of silence which came upon them. They were dumfounded and speechless in the presence of such unparalleled suffering.

What could they say? How could they speak? For "they saw that his pain was very great" (2:13, mg.).

Job's Complaint

> "After this opened Job his mouth, and cursed his day." (Job 3:1)

Job was the first to break the silence, and when he speaks he pours out the depths of his soul. There was no renouncing of God, no word of rebellion against His hand upon him, but he "curses" the day of his birth. The word is quite a different one in the original to the word "renounce" in the previous passages. It means simply that he "execrated" his day.

He has spoken no word of welcome to his friends, explained nothing to them, for formalities and ordinary language have no place at such a time.

The words that Job pours out in the anguish of his soul tell us something of the thoughts which have been filling his mind in these hours of silence.

"*Let the day perish wherein I was born,*" he cries. "That anniversary of my birth, which is ordinarily to be kept as a joyous festival, let it henceforth be regarded as a day of mourning. Oh that it could be blotted out from the calendar, that it might be forgotten—miserable day!" (3:3-10).

"*Why died I not* [*in my mother's*] *womb?* . . . For now should I have lain down and been quiet . . . [and] at rest" (3:11-13).

"I would now be sleeping," says Job, with kings

who have had to leave their "palaces which now lie in ruins" (3:14, mg.) which they built for themselves on earth. I would be with princes who have had to part with their gold.

In the grave the weary have rest, the wicked cease from raging, the prisoners are at ease from the task-master, and the servant is free—for both the small and the great are there (3:17–19).

Strangely, the soul often turns to thoughts of death in the hour of deep trial. "It is enough . . . take away my life," said Elijah to the Lord in his time of exhaustion under the juniper tree. "It is too heavy for me; kill me, I pray Thee," said Moses under the pressure of the burden of the people. "It is better for me to die," said Jonah, when the Lord did not fulfill the threatened judgment upon Nineveh. Many have said again and again in their time of anguish, "I wish I were dead."

Job had not rebelled against the Lord, but he was coming perilously close to doing so in using this language. He had told his wife that we should be willing to "*endure evil things*" as well as receive "*good things*" from the hand of God (Septuagint). But to "long for death" as the way of escape from evil is not the way to bow to the will of God. It is merely the cry of nature for escape from suffering—pressed out from the soul in its anguish and pain.

The Adversary is at the back of much of this language from the lips of Job, even as he was the instigator of the temptation to speak against God that came to him from the lips of his dear wife.

It is the enemy that is throwing this cloud upon Job's soul and pouring into his mind these thoughts of escape through death. There are people who have yielded to such thoughts in the time of deep anguish and ultimately have been driven by the tempter to take their lives in order to reach this place of rest.

Let God's children take heed and stand firm upon their God, thanking Him for the *privilege* of life. Let them turn from the temptation of dwelling upon the peace of the grave and choose *life*, even though it be life in the very crucible of fire, for "the sky, not the grave, is our goal."

Having deplored his personal situation, Job now raises the philosophical question, "Why does God let men go on living in misery? Especially those who are longing for death and search for it as a treasure?" (3:20-22).

As Job cries, he does not realize the cowardice of his language nor how he is opening the door to the enemy of his soul. He goes on to call himself a man "*whom God hath hedged in*" (3:23), including among his miseries what the devil had called his peculiar blessing—God's encompassing!

Job concludes this outpouring of his grief by saying, "*The thing which I feared is come upon me*" (3:25, mg.).

Taught of God as Job was, he knew that the testing time must come. He had shrunk from it and been afraid of it. He confesses that he had not been at ease (3:26, mg.) in spite of the outward peace of his life. He had known that the furnace was inevitable, and now all that he had shrunk from had come upon him.

CHAPTER 3

"It was not an enemy that reproached me. . . . But it was thou, . . . my companion, and my familiar friend." (Psalm 55:12–13)

ELIPHAZ' FIRST APPEAL, AND JOB'S REPLY

"Then answered Eliphaz the Temanite, and said. . . . " (Job 4:1)

ELIPHAZ is the first of the three friends to speak. We may describe him as the "candid friend," the friend we know so well in actual life who always feels it incumbent upon him to speak out all his mind!

We have seen how the three men made an appointment together to come and comfort Job. Discussing the sad news, they had settled among themselves the only way in which he could be really helped out of his troubles—and Eliphaz is the one chosen for the delicate task of suggesting to him the conclusions they had come to.

Eliphaz begins by saying, "If I try to speak to you, Job, will you be grieved? But who could keep from speaking after listening to all you have said" (4:2). Then he goes on to put into plain, bald language the bitterest thought of all, a thought that possibly had been rankling in Job's mind while he was speaking: "Behold thou hast instructed many, . . . thou hast strengthened the weak, . . . thou hast confirmed the feeble knees. But now it is come unto *thee,* and thou faintest; it toucheth *thee,* and thou art troubled" (4:3–5).

It must be confessed that Job had given cause to Eliphaz to say all this, and Eliphaz probably expressed the thought of them all in the words he uses. "Job, Job, you have taught others, helped them with your words, strengthened and upheld those that were falling, and *now*—when you are put into the same circumstances—we see *you* fainting and troubled!"

Did not Job know all this in his heart? Did not the Adversary anticipate the words of Eliphaz and whisper all this to Job when he was sinking under his misery? As the words about death and the grave came out of his lips, did he not *know* that he was fainting under the hand of God, and did not the memory of the way he had instructed others add agony to his fainting spirit? But it was bitter pain to have the keen-eyed Eliphaz put all this into cold, bare words.

"*Is not thy fear of God thy confidence?*" continues Eliphaz (4:6). "Job, *you* of all men should know how to trust God in the hour of trial! Is not your knowledge of Him sufficient to give you confidence now?"

Oh dear soul in the furnace, are these not like the words of some who have tried to console you? They have spoken about the grief of the one whom *God* has wounded, and offer "comfort" by saying, "*Remember, you told others, 'Be strong,'* and now you yourself are fainting."

The Candid Friend's "Comfort"

"Remember, . . . who ever perished, being innocent? . . . According as I have seen, they that plow iniquity, and sow trouble, reap the same." (Job 4:7–8)

This is "comfort" from the candid friend! Eliphaz draws upon his long experience and says that he has seen that men simply *reap what they sow.*

In plain language, the suggestion is that Job must

be reaping the consequences of sin. Surely, none have ever perished or been brought to such extremity as *he* is in when they were innocent! *God must be angry with him* (4:9).

Eliphaz could say this with conviction and assurance, for he was not speaking out of his own mind but as one taught by God. He would tell Job how this knowledge had come to him: "Now a thing was secretly brought to me . . . in . . . *visions of the night.* . . . A spirit passed before my face. . . . A form was before mine eyes. . . . I heard a still voice, saying, Shall mortal man be just before God? Shall a man be pure before his Maker?" (4:12–17, mg.).

Eliphaz seeks to enforce his words with the account of a "vision" which had come to him in the night; but the language of the spirit-form that passed before his eyes savors more of the *devil* appearing as an angel of light than of the Holy Spirit of God.

The Adversary who had accused Job to God before the heavenly assembly and asserted that in the crucible he would unfailingly renounce his faith in Him was not likely to leave any means untried on earth to bring about the end which he desired.

In reading Job's story, we must bear in mind continually the forces that lie behind the surface history. The Adversary had set his heart upon Job, and his tactics are not ended when he has stripped him of all his possessions and stricken him down to the ground. He attacks him through his wife's words, then by dangling before him the thought of escaping into the grave, and now through the lips of the three friends—particularly at this stage, by the words of Eliphaz. Every point is thus seen to be a direct attack against the "integrity" of Job, his faith in God and his assurance of fellowship with Him.

Eliphaz asserts that he has learned through a spirit-vision that no mortal man can be just and pure before his Maker. He says in effect, "Job, you had better *let go* your confidence that you have walked with God in integrity of heart. Your present experience proves that you are just the same as other men! You thought that God protected and blessed you, but after all, you are reaping the consequences of sin just as others do! You shun evil, you say, and seek to walk uprightly; but no man can be counted just before God, no man can be pure before his Maker."

"*Behold, [God] putteth no trust in His servants; and His angels He chargeth with folly. How much more them that dwell in houses of clay?*" whispers the spirit voice to Eliphaz at the very time that Jehovah was trusting His servant Job with the fullest confidence He could have placed in him. God, instead of charging him with "folly," had borne witness before the council of heaven that in His sight Job was "blameless and true and godly, abstaining from everything evil" (Job 1:8, Septuagint).

The Adversary is always accusing man to God and God to man, maligning the Creator's character and misrepresenting His attitude toward the creatures He has made. "*Man is only like a moth,*" said this spirit to Eliphaz. "He is crushed in one brief day; he perishes and none regard it" (4:19–20, mg.).

Alas for those who rely upon spirit-visions for knowledge about God! They are bound to be led astray. This "lying spirit" has wholly misled Eliphaz and deceived him with a half-truth. It is true that mortal man is not pure before the Holy God, but the spirit voice said nothing about the "*sacrifice,*" the burnt offerings which Job offered continually, and which in the foreknowledge of God anticipated the sacrifice of Christ upon Calvary's cross, in whom and through whom a man stands accepted before his Maker.

That man's life on earth may be said to be as brief

as the life of a *moth* is also true; but that God lets him perish unregarded is *untrue*. For the Son of God, who came to declare the Father, said to His disciples, "The very hairs of your head are all numbered. . . . Ye are of more value than many sparrows" (Matthew 10:30–31).

"*Call now,*" said Eliphaz to his afflicted friend, "*is there any that will answer thee? And to which of the holy ones wilt thou turn?*" (5:1).

These words imply that Eliphaz was under the impression that the spirit-form which had passed before his face was one of the "holy ones," an angel of God. *Unto which of the holy ones* would Job turn for help and counsel in his trouble?

"*As for me,*" said Eliphaz, "*I would seek unto God, and unto God would I commit my cause*" (5:8), thus showing that he had not discerned the devil as an angel of light in the vision which had come to him.

There are *many* like Eliphaz in these days. Some would use his very words in describing "things secretly brought to them" in the stillness of the night— communications from the spirit-world which they fully believe to be *messages from God*. Oh, they have no intention of forsaking the Lord any more than Eliphaz had but think that by this means they will get to know Him better. May God open their eyes to the devices of the evil one and deliver them from his snare!

I have seen all this in experience, continues Eliphaz. "*I have seen the foolish taking root; but suddenly I cursed his habitation. His children are . . . crushed in the gate with none to deliver them*" (5:3–4).

What attitude does Eliphaz reveal here? The vision of the night he speaks of has clearly not resulted in the manifestation of that spirit of pity and love which comes from fellowship with the God of *love*.

"Affliction cometh not forth of the dust, neither

doth trouble spring out of the ground" (5:6) is the callous reasoning of Eliphaz. He had spoken a "curse" against the "foolish," and the consequence had followed. Therefore, he concludes, there must also be some cause for *Job's* trouble.

If I were in your place, Job, Eliphaz continues, *I* would commit my cause to God. He does great things, marvelous things without number (5:9). He sets on high those who are lowly and lifts up those who are mourning to a place of safety (5:11). He frustrates the devices of the crafty and catches the wise in their own craftiness (5:12–13). He saves the needy from the hand of the mighty, so that the poor have hope (5:15–16).

The Exhortation of Eliphaz

> "Behold, happy is the man whom God reproveth. . . . Despise not thou the chastening of El-Shaddai. For He maketh sore, and bindeth up: He woundeth, and His hands make whole." (Job 5:17–18, mg.)

Eliphaz appears to be a strange mixture. He undoubtedly has some knowledge of God, whether by *theory* or otherwise we cannot say. After his first words in answer to Job's complaint of his condition, he has dealt with him very gently. He only *suggests* that men reap what they sow and sincerely advises Job to seek God for deliverance from his trouble. Job should think himself *happy* to be corrected by God; it will be well for him not to despise His chastening. If El-Shaddai—the Pourer-forth of blessing—makes sore, He just as surely binds up; if He wounds, He unfailingly makes whole.

From this piece of advice Eliphaz goes on to draw a most beautiful picture of the result of the *binding up* by the hands of the Almighty. If Job would but truly seek Him and not despise His chastening, El-Shaddai would deliver him from every trouble that might come upon him so that *no evil should touch him* (5:19). In famine he would be kept from death; in war he would be *saved from the sword* (5:20). The *scourge of the tongue* would not touch him; he would not be *afraid of destruction* (5: 21). He would *laugh at every danger* and be fearless before the beasts of the field (5:22–23). His home would be in peace and protected by the power of God (5:24). His offspring would be as the grass, and he would come to his grave in a full age like a "*shock of corn in its season*" (5:25–26).

"*Lo this, we have searched it, so it is,*" adds Eliphaz. So hear it and apply it to yourself, Job, for we sincerely desire your good (5:27).

Very beautiful, Eliphaz, but this is not the appropriate time! "*A wise man's heart discerneth time and judgment.*" It was not the *time* for Eliphaz to urge the blessings of deliverance. The premise also was wrong. All this would be *if* Job would go back to God, but Job *had not left Him!* Eliphaz did not understand!

Job's Reply

"Then Job answered and said. . . ." (Job 6:1)

Job listens, but the words of Eliphaz do not reach his soul. He does not hear with the inner ear because of his anguish of spirit. He breaks out that if his calamity could be weighed, it would be found to be "heavier than the sand of the seas" (6:2–3). "*The arrows of the Almighty are within me,*" he cries, the "*terrors of God*" are set in array against me (6:4).

The beasts make a cry of distress over their food when it is unpalatable (6:5); just so am I bound to cry out in my sufferings, for nature must be allowed relief. Because of my distress, all food is "saltless"— like the white of an egg. I have no appetite (6:6–7).

Eliphaz, *you* say that men can be destroyed like moths. If only God would grant me what I long for—I wish it would please Him to crush *me!* If He would but let loose His hand and cut me off, then I should have comfort. And my joy during the pain would be that I had not denied the words of the Holy One (6:8–10, mg.).

What strength have I now to wait for deliverance, and what have I to look forward to that I should be patient? I am not made of brass to endure all this. I am completely helpless, and recovery is driven from me (6:11–13).

Job's Disappointment

"To him who is ready to faint, *kindness* should be shown from his friend; else might he forsake . . . the fear of the Almighty." (Job 6:14, mg.)

Job says that Eliphaz had come professedly to comfort him, but he had not dealt kindly with him. He had reproached him with fainting under the hand of God after teaching and helping others. Granted that it was so, "to him who is ready to faint" his friend should show *kindness*, not severity! Otherwise the fainting one might be driven away from God altogether.

Job compares his friends to an undependable brook—sometimes choked with dirty ice and snow, and sometimes completely dry—and graphically pictures the disappointment of the caravans in the desert when turning aside to seek water in their hour of need (6:15–21).

"*Ye are like thereto*" (6:21, mg.), cries Job. "You have given me no comfort from the heart of God, you frozen streams; you see me so loathsome that I am a terror to you, and *you are afraid to be kind to me,* lest you be accounted a partaker of the sins you charge me with."

Job's Appeal to His Friends

> "Did I say, Give unto me? . . . Or, Deliver me? . . .
> Or, Redeem me from the hand of the oppressors? . . .
> Teach me, and I will hold my peace." (Job 6:22–24)

Smarting from the pain of disappointment in those who should have understood and helped him by true heart sympathy in his time of trial, Job reminds Eliphaz that he had asked nothing of him or those with him! He had not asked for a gift from their substance, although he had lost everything; nor had he cried to *them* to deliver him from the oppressor.

Job declares that he is quite willing to be taught and to be made to understand wherein he may have erred (6:24). Honest words carry force and weight, but the arguing of Eliphaz has had no power. What is he arguing about? What is he trying to accomplish by his reproof? He has treated the speeches of a desperate man as nothing but wind—mere words! (6:25–26, mg.).

"Yea," cries Job, *"ye would cast lots upon the fatherless"* (6:27), so hardhearted are you. A man who could deal as you have dealt with me in my pitiable condition would be capable of selling his best friend.

"Be pleased to look at me; it will be evident unto you if I am lying to your face. Is there injustice on my tongue?" (6:28–30, mg.). Job maintains that his character should not be judged by them, nor should his friends charge him in his bitter anguish with reaping what he had sown.

Job's Pitiful State

> "Is there not a warfare to man upon earth? . . . So am I made to possess months of misery and wearisome nights. . . . I am full of tossings. . . . My flesh is clothed with worms and clods of dust; my skin is broken and become loathsome." (Job 7:1–5, mg.)

Job is feeling very keenly the evident lack of understanding in his friends. His condition was sufficient to melt the hardest heart; but Eliphaz and his companions had settled that Job *must be dealt with as a transgressor*, and to give him *sympathy* when he was an evident evildoer would only injure him seriously in his soul and make his friends partakers of his sins.

Job now compares his days to those of a hired man, even to those of a conscript in the army. *"Is there not a warfare to man upon earth? And are not his days like the days of an hireling?"* (7:1). He is under authority and has to accept all that is appointed for him. There is a "time of service" for every man, when he has to learn obedience to the will of God before he can be trusted with authority in the Kingdom of God.

"I am in that warfare," Job says. "I am appointed wearisome nights, tossings to and fro until the dawning of the day; months of weary waiting instead of happy service" (7:3–4).

He describes himself further: "My skin is broken and become loathsome (7:5); my life is passing as rapidly as the shuttle in the weaver's hand (7:6). Oh Eliphaz, remember my life is like the wind (7:7); I am passing from your sight; you will look for me and I shall be gone (7:8). Like a cloud I shall vanish away; I shall return no more to my home; my place shall be empty: therefore I must speak in the anguish of my spirit. It is useless talking to me about going to my grave in a full age like a shock of corn; I am a dying man, and I must pour out the bitterness of my soul (7:9–11)."

Job's Complaint to God

"Am I . . . a sea-monster, that Thou settest a watch over me? . . . Let me alone. . . . What is man that Thou shouldest magnify him, and that Thou shouldest set Thine heart upon him . . . and try him every moment?" (Job 7:12-18)

From his would-be comforters Job turns to God and almost petulantly cries, "Am I . . . a sea-monster, that You set a guard over me?" His terrible nights of suffering seem the keenest point of his complaint—those awful nights of tossing to and fro until the dawning of the day. When he goes to his couch in hope of some relief from his pain, then he is scared by dreams and fearful visions. Was Job right in charging God with these? Were they not part of the enemy's devices? However, such awful nights made him feel that strangling would be a mercy (7:15). He could not but loathe his life; he did not want to live in such a warfare as this (7:16).

"*Let me alone,*" he cries to God. Why should You magnify frail man by setting Your heart upon him, visiting him and testing him every moment? Oh that You would turn away Your eyes from me (7:17-19)! "*If I have sinned, what can I do unto Thee, O Thou watcher of men? . . . Why dost Thou not pardon my transgression?*" If iniquity that I know not of is the cause of all this suffering, why do You not take it away?—for I soon shall lie down in the dust and shall not be (7:20-21, mg.).

CHAPTER 4

"Behold, . . . I have chosen thee in the furnace of affliction." (Isaiah 48:10)

BILDAD'S REASONING, AND JOB'S CRY FOR A MEDIATOR

"Then answered Bildad the Shuhite, and said. . . ." (Job 8:1)

THE distinctive character of each of the three friends of Job is revealed very strikingly in their different speeches and varying methods of dealing with Job. Eliphaz was possibly considered the most "spiritual" of the three, perhaps on account of his assurance that he had been taught by God in visions of the night. Maybe for this reason he was chosen to speak to Job first. He is also the one who deals the plainest with him in charging him with definite transgressions.

Bildad may be described as the very "humble" friend. He speaks the least of the three, always mildly, within a narrow scope, and generally as a gentle echo of the other two men.

Bildad had listened to all that passed between Eliphaz and Job. He had heard Job's cry to God, "If I have sinned, . . . why dost Thou not pardon my transgression?" and he now proceeds to reason gently with him.

"How long, Job, will you speak like this? Does El-Shaddai pervert justice? If you know not of any iniquity in your *own* life, perhaps *your children* have

51

sinned, and God has delivered them to the consequences of their sin. Your *children* have been rightly
punished for their transgressions" (8:2-4).

"Oh, Job, *if* you would but seek earnestly unto God
and make your supplication unto El-Shaddai—the
Pourer-forth of blessing. *If* you were pure and upright, surely now He would awake for you and make
you prosperous" (8:5-6).

Here is the sting. This terrible "*If,*" so full of torture
to the soul in the crucible. The devil whispers, "*If* all
were right with God, He would deliver you!" The
gentle friend who comes to assist in the time of
trouble suggests again, "*If* all were clear with God,
would He not interpose and set you free?" The perplexed soul itself cries, "*If* I have sinned against
You—but why this?"

No loss of earth's possessions, no misjudgment of
friends, no physical suffering can compare with the
pain aroused by that "if" in one who has walked with
God in integrity.

Bildad has studied the "teaching of the fathers."
Eliphaz had based *his* knowledge upon spirit-teach-
ing from the other world, but Bildad would not presume to rely on that; he is satisfied to accept the
authority of antiquity. He has a great reverence for
tradition. He does not venture to assume that he
knows anything novel at all (8:8-9)!

The fathers had long ago searched out the truth,
and they had settled the fact that God prospers all
who are upright and punishes all who are ungodly.
Suffering is invariably the result of sin, prosperity
the reward of innocence. Surely Job should bow his
head and accept the teaching of *authority.* Was he
going to presume that he knew God better than
others of the former age (8:10)?

Bildad was only an "echo," like many people today.
He was content to take his knowledge secondhand. It

looked like humility. Better and wiser men than he had said these things, and he was satisfied to accept their conclusions.

After this appeal to tradition, Bildad draws for Job a picture of the paths of those who forget God (8:13). His illustrations are drawn from a small area: the withered papyrus (8:11–12), the spider's web (8:14), the poorly-constructed house (8:15), the uprooted plant in the garden (8:16–18)—all showing that his sphere had probably been a very circumscribed one, and his mind and vision had remained correspondingly small.

Bildad's Encouragement

"Behold, God will not cast away a perfect man. . . . He will yet fill thy mouth with laughter, and thy lips with shouting." (Job 8:20–21)

Bildad is a kind man and in his way feels sorry for poor Job. He would like to give him a word of cheer. All that he has said about the fate of the godless is true; so if Job will only get right with God, God will not cast him off but will yet fill his mouth with laughter and shouting.

Hardly a suitable word to buoy up the formerly dignified patriarch who sat as chief among his people!

Bildad's idea of encouragement reminds us of well-intentioned friends in modern days who say, "Come, cheer up. We'll see you laughing and shouting before long!"

Bildad meant it kindly, but deep anguish of soul is not so easily dismissed. His small and shallow mind is not capable of realizing the depths of a man like Job.

"*They that hate thee shall be clothed with shame*" (8:22), adds this would-be comforter. What! A man of the character of Job cheered by the thought of seeing

others humiliated? It might be some comfort to a
man of Bildad's stamp, but to one who had walked in
fellowship with God—never!

Job's Reply to Bildad

> "Then Job answered and said, Of a truth I know
> that it is so: but *how* can man be just before God?"
> (Job 9:1-2, mg.)

Bildad's humble attitude and gentle reasoning have
soothed the suffering Job, and he quietly answers
him, *"Truly I know that it is so."*

All that Bildad has said about God not upholding
evildoers is quite true, and Job is willing to acknowledge it. The words of Eliphaz, however, remain in his
mind, especially the question propounded by the
spirit-voice: *"Shall mortal man be just before God?"*
(4:17).

"How can man be just before God?" Job now repeats. The question may not have occurred to him
before. He only knew that he had walked with God in
integrity of heart and that the friendship of God has
been given him. In obedience to the Lord he had
offered up sacrifices, but as to "how" he was justified
before Him he did not know.

From the spirit-vision given to Eliphaz, we gather
that it is the Adversary who suggests the "*shall*" and
the "*how.*" His one object is to prevent or to break
communion between the soul and its God. Let the
intellect be occupied with the "*how*" and the soul will
generally fail to know deep fellowship with God in
experience.

Job appears to be in the position of one who has
been having happy and close fellowship with God but
is suddenly asked "How?" Such a question can be a
severe test to a trusting heart. He has been so happy
in his blessed child-like walk with God. What does

this strange unbelief in the world around him mean? Why is he being disturbed by those who want indefinable things defined? Why are they not content to take the word of the Lord? Can he not simply be left alone to walk with his God? *Must* he be able to answer the "*How*"?

It is all part of the refining fire. The very foundations are being tried. Through testing, the soul will learn how to give a reason for the hope it possesses, with meekness and fear.

Job has been thinking over this question of being "just before God," and in answer to Bildad he pours out the thoughts passing through his mind.

"*How* can a man be just before God?" If one wished to dispute with God, he could not answer Him one time out of a thousand. Consider His wisdom and strength. He is so mighty that He overturns mountains, shakes the earth out of its place, commands the sun to set, stretches out the heavens, treads upon the stormy sea, designs the constellations; yes, He does marvelous things, *great things past finding out* (9:3–10). This great God, so invisible, so all-powerful—who can rebuke Him or say, "*What doest Thou?*" (9:11–12).

How then could I, Job, possibly speak to Him or reason with Him? Though I were fully righteous, I could not converse with Him; for He is God and I am but a man. If I summoned Him and He answered me, I could not believe that He had hearkened to my voice! He who is crushing me with a tempest of trouble, multiplying my wounds—without cause it seems to me—and does not allow me time to take my breath but fills me with bitterness (9:14–18), how could I argue with Him?

It appears from this language that Job did not yet know God as the One who *talked with him.* He knew Him more in his inner consciousness as the great

Holy One before whom he walked in integrity of heart, shunning evil, and fearing Him with godly awe. Job little suspected that this path of suffering was to end in a revelation of God and a fellowship with Him *richer* and *fuller* than anything he had ever conceived of in his days of prosperity!

As Job compares himself with the omnipotent God, he is brought to despair. If he considers relative strength, there is no hope; if the topic is "justice," who will appoint the place of meeting for him to plead (9:19)? Even if he were innocent and maintained he was perfect, Jehovah would prove him perverse (9:20). No, the matter is hopeless; he cannot justify himself, he simply despises himself and his life. "It is all one thing; therefore *I* say, *He destroyeth the perfect and the wicked*" (9:22). *You* say, Bildad, that God will not cast away a perfect man; but as I think of His omnipotence and see Him using His power to crush me to pieces, *I* say it is all foolish talk! No man can be just before God if it requires one's justification of himself! The "perfect" and the wicked stand in the same place; in fact, it appears as if God actually mocks at the calamity of the innocent and hands over the good of the earth to the wicked. If it is not *God* who controls all these things, then who is it (9:23–24)?

You tell me, Bildad, to *"brighten up"* (9:27, mg.); but if I try to forget my complaint and "be of good cheer," I am still haunted by all my sorrows and know that God will *not* hold me innocent (9:28).

You tell me that if I were pure and upright He would surely work on my behalf, but what can I do? I have appealed to Him to pardon any transgression; it is labor in vain for me to try and wash myself. If I were to cleanse my hands with lye (9:30, mg.), He would, so to speak, plunge me into the ditch again (9:31).

Job's Cry for a Mediator

> "He is not a man, as I am, . . . that we should come together in judgment. There is no umpire betwixt us."
> (Job 9:32–33, mg.)

Job is getting lower and lower before God. The distance between the Creator and the finite creature that He has made is so great. Oh that there were an umpire between us, Job cries, one who could "*lay his hand upon us both!*"

The need of the human heart has always been the same. Job knew how to offer burnt offerings unto God and through them to understand that he was accepted by Him; but in his hour of need, when God appeared so far off, he longs for an umpire between Jehovah and himself—someone who could both plead with God for him and speak to him from God.

When life and immortality were brought to light through the gospel, it was revealed that God *had* met this cry by the gift of His only begotten Son, who became the "one Mediator between God and man, Himself man—Christ Jesus" (1 Timothy 2:5); and "it behoved Him in all things to be made like unto His brethren, that He might be a merciful and faithful high priest in things pertaining to God, to make propitiation for the sins of the people" (Hebrews 2:17).

Job cries again, "Let Him take His rod away. . . . *Then would I speak, and not fear Him; for I am not so in myself*" (9:34–35). I am not afraid of God *in my heart*, but "while I suffer [His] terrors I am distracted." I am so weary of my life that I must give "free course to my complaint" and "speak in the bitterness of my soul"—I *will* plead with God, he declares (10:1).

Job's Appeal to God

"Do not condemn me: show me wherefore Thou contendest with me. Is it good . . . that Thou shouldest oppress [and] despise the labour of Thine hands?" (Job 10:2–3, mg.)

The words that follow may well be described as "a prayer of the afflicted when he fainteth, and poureth out his complaint before the Lord." *

Job's pleading with God is very touching. "*Show me wherefore Thou contendest with me,*" he cries. Is it Your good pleasure to oppress and despise Your handiwork? Do You see merely as *man* sees (10:3–4)? Are You judging me like these men, and searching me for some secret sin when You, the One who knows all hearts, *knows* that I am not wicked (10:5–7)?

I am in Your hands, Lord. You have fashioned me, and yet You are destroying me. "*Wilt Thou bring me into dust again*" (10:8–9)? You have made me. You have given me life. You have preserved me, and yet You have had all this suffering hidden in Your heart for me (10:11–13)!

I know Your character enough to know, Lord, that You will not overlook any transgression in Your children. You will not acquit me of any iniquity. If You see anything that is "wicked" then it will be "*woe unto me*" (10:14–15), and You will deal severely with me. If I be righteous before You, Lord, I still cannot "lift up my head; *I am filled with ignominy*" (10:15, mg.). If for a moment I do raise my head, You spring upon me as a lion hunts its prey, and again You show Your awesome power against me (10:16).

Oh Lord, Your indignation seems to increase, and "*host after host is against me*" (10:17, mg.). Why did You let me live at my birth? If I had died, no eye

---

* Psalm 102. Head-note and margin.

would have seen me now as I am (10:18–19).

"*Are not my days few?*" Will You not "*let me alone*
that I may take comfort a little, before I go to the *land
of darkness and of the shadow of death*; a land of
thick darkness, as darkness itself?" (10:20–22).

CHAPTER 5

"The proof of your faith, being more precious than gold that perisheth, though it is proved by fire. . . ." (1 Peter 1:7)

ZOPHAR'S FIRST SPEECH, AND JOB'S VENTURE OF FAITH

"Then answered Zophar the Naamathite, and said, Should not the multitude of words be answered? And should a man full of talk be justified?" (Job 11:1–2).

ZOPHAR, the third friend, is thought to be the oldest of the three men and to speak with the tone of extreme age. This may account for his blunt, almost rough language to a man of Job's position and character.

Eliphaz had only hinted to Job the conclusions they had come to, and Bildad had gently echoed his words by saying, "*If you were pure and upright, God would surely awake for you.*"

Zophar now roughly and bluntly breaks out, "*Should a man full of talk be justified?*" His indignation has been growing as he listens to Job pleading with God and saying that he knows of no cause for his affliction but longs for an umpire to stand as judge between Jehovah and himself.

Zophar does not mince his words. He considers it is time that Job was spoken to a little more plainly. Gentle dealing is evidently in vain, for he thinks that Job is "full of talk" and "boasting." It is only mockery for Job to appeal to God in the way he has done and to persist in saying that his conscience is clear before Him (11:2–4).

Zophar feels indignation on God's behalf; he wishes that God would open His lips against such mockery and show Job that He was exacting of him even less than his iniquity deserved (11:5–6)!

How a man should speak so boldly to Jehovah was beyond his comprehension. Did Job not realize the greatness of the God to whom he was appealing so freely?

Was Job, as a man, able to know the deep things of God (11:7)? Could he find out El-Shaddai to perfection? God's infinitude is as the heights of heaven and the depth of the grave, longer than the earth and broader than the sea (11:8–9). But El-Shaddai knows vain men; He can see iniquity, even though a man considers it not (11:11).

What use, though, to talk to Job? *"An empty man will get understanding,"* Zophar contemptuously says, only *"when a wild ass's colt is born a man"* (11:12, mg.)!

Zophar's Exhortation

> "If thou set thine heart aright, and stretch out thine hands toward Him; if iniquity be in thine hand, put it far away. . . . Surely then. . . ." (Job 11:13–15)

"If you were pure and upright, surely He would awake for you," said Bildad; and Zophar continues on the same text. *If* you would set your heart right. *If* you would but truly cry to Jehovah and put iniquity away from you (11:13–14), surely then, Job, *then* you could lift up your head and be without fear (11:5).

If you will but put things right, Job, *then* you shall *forget your misery,* and *remember it as waters that are passed away* (11:16); your life shall *arise above the noonday*; the darkness shall be changed into the light of morning (11:17); you shall *take your rest in safety* (11:18) without these terrible dreams you speak of; you shall *lie down* without fear. Yes, you shall be restored to your place of dignity and authority, and *many shall entreat your favor* (11:19).

But the wicked have no place to flee; there is no hope for *them* but death (11:20)!

Job's Reply to Zophar

> "Then Job answered, . . . No doubt but ye are the people, and wisdom shall die with you." (Job 12:1-2)

A blunt friend is often a blessing! Job had only winced under the reproachful sarcasm and assumed spiritual authority of Eliphaz. In answer he had expressed bitter disappointment at his lack of kindness and sympathy with him in his affliction, and then he poured out a pathetic account of his pitiable condition, as a man manifestly drawing near to the grave.

Under Bildad's gentle reasoning and evident desire to encourage him, Job had almost sunk into despair as he dwelt upon the omnipotence of God and faced the question of *how* to be counted just before Him. He had nevertheless poured out his heart in pleading with this great Jehovah, but had sunk again into the wail that his days were but few and that he was a dying man.

But the rough language of Zophar acts like a tonic. It stirs him to a vigorous reply, awakens the faith that is lying dormant in him, and rouses it to a tenacious hold on God that will carry him through his trial.

The "dying man" has more vigor in his soul than he knows. He answers Zophar as bluntly as he had spoken to him. Sarcastically he says, "No doubt but *ye are the people, and wisdom shall die with you!* But

I have understanding as well as you; I am not inferior
to you: . . . *who knoweth not such things as these?"*
(12:2–3). Zophar, you are making me a "laughing-
stock" to talk to me like this! *I,* who have in the past
called upon God and received His answer. The "just
man"—the man that has walked with God and known
that he was accepted of Him—is being *laughed at* by
his neighbor (12:4)!

Those who prosper and live *at ease* show contempt
for misfortune (12:5), cries the stricken man.

Job is as blunt as Zophar when he says, *"Ask now
the beasts, and they shall teach thee!"* Who does not
know that in the hand of the Lord is the life of every
living thing (12:7–10)?

Zophar had spoken of the greatness of God, but all
nature bore witness to this. The ear could test words,
even as the palate tasted meat, and Job could not
discern any extraordinary light in Zophar's language
(12:11).

"With aged men, ye say, *is wisdom"* (v. 12, mg.),
but I say that *"wisdom and might"* is with *God* (12:13),
continues Job. The God that he had pleaded with
was the One who works all things after the counsel of
His own will; it was He *alone* who has understanding.

God breaks things down so effectually that anything He breaks cannot be built up again. He shuts
up a man, and no one can open the doors for him
when God holds the key (12:14).

He holds back the floods of water, and again He
lets them loose so that they devastate the earth; *to
Him belong strength and victory* (12:15–16).

Jehovah is the sovereign Lord of all. He takes away
the wisdom of the wise (12:17); He binds and makes
loose even kings (12:18); He overthrows the mighty
(12:19); He takes away speech and discernment from
the aged (12:20) and pours contempt upon princes

(12:21); He brings out the riches of darkness (12:22); He increases or decreases nations and works His will upon the highest of the people of the earth (12:23–25).

Job's Desire

"Surely I would speak to the Almighty, and I desire to reason with God." (Job 13:3)

Zophar had wished that God would open His lips against Job, but Job was not afraid of this; he desired with all his soul to speak with God. He repeats that he is not inferior to Zophar in knowledge of Jehovah (13:2); his friends had come professedly to help him, but they were *"physicians of no value"*; he would even describe them as *"forgers of lies"* (13:4), for they were charging him with things that were utterly untrue. What use is a physician who cannot diagnose the case? It would show more wisdom if they were to acknowledge their ignorance and remain silent (13:5).

His friends had sought to reason with Job; let them now listen to his reasoning with them (13:6). They had sought to contend for God (13:8). What mockery! The Lord would surely reprove them for showing partiality in their hearts (13:9–10). They would not have spoken to Job in his days of authority like they have spoken to him while an outcast upon the ash-heap. Were they not afraid thus to deal with a servant of God (13:11)? Their "memorable sayings" were but ashes, and their excuses, "defenses of clay" (13:12).

They had better keep silent and let him alone; he *would* speak, let the consequences be what they may (13:13)!

Job's Venture of Faith

> "Whatever the risk, I will take . . . my life in mine
> hand" (13:14, mg.). "Though He slay me, yet will I trust
> in Him. . . . I will maintain mine own ways before Him.
> He also shall be my salvation." (Job 13:15–16, A.V.)

Job is thoroughly aroused by Zophar's harshness
and is driven to a desperate venture of faith. Whatever the cost, he will take his life in his hand and
cast himself upon the character of God. He will trust
God even though He pleases to slay him. He will hold
to it that, almighty as Jehovah is, he may argue his
case with Him and the Lord Himself will be his
salvation.

He is sure that a hypocrite will not be permitted to
enter His presence (13:16, A.V.), and in the hearing
of his friends he will "order his cause" before Him.
Although he may not be able to say *how* a man may
be counted just before God, yet he *knows* that he
"*shall be justified*" (13:17–18, mg.).

Looking upon his would-be helpers, Job asks if
there are any that will venture to further contend
with him. He is in such a state that if he keeps silent
he feels he will die (13:19).

There are only two things he will ask of the Lord,
and then he will shrink away from His face (13:20).
"*Withdraw Thine hand*," he cries to God, "*and let not
Thy terror make me afraid. Then call Thou, and I will
answer; or let me speak, and answer Thou me*"
(13:21–22).

Job has referred to this "terror" once before. "Knowing the *terror of the Lord*, we persuade men," said the
Apostle Paul in writing to the Corinthians long after
the time of Job. Without question *there is a revelation of God as the One terrible in holiness*, even to the
redeemed, so that they might know the exceeding
sinfulness of sin and fear Him with godly awe.

"While I suffer *Thy terrors* I am distracted . . . *Thy terrors* have cut me off," cried David (Psalm 88:15–16), when in the same crucible as Job.

Job's Appeal to God

"How many are mine iniquities and sins? *Make me to know* my transgression and my sin." (Job 13:23)

Job's friends are charging him with reaping what he has sown and telling him that he is suffering even less than his iniquity deserves; but he turns from them and once more pours out his soul to the Lord. Will He not make him *know* what these iniquities are? *Why* does he hide His face and treat him as an enemy (13:24)? Will the great God "harass a driven leaf"? Will He, the Mighty One, ceaselessly pursue a wisp of "dry stubble" (13:25)?

Job goes back in searching of heart to his early days. Is the All-seeing God making him to "inherit the iniquities of [his] youth"? He is putting him in the "stocks" looking narrowly at all his paths, as it were, *drawing a line about the soles of his feet,* so that every step he takes is marked (13:27). He feels like a "rotten thing," a "moth-eaten" garment, only fit to be thrown aside (13:28); and yet he does not know of any definite "iniquity" or "transgression" to cause this terrible dealing by God.

Job's Question

"If a man die, shall he live again?" (Job 14:14)

After his appeal to God, Job's thought turns to the frailty of human life, and the words he uses make it appear that as yet he had no *clear* assurance of the life to come.

Job evidently feels that he is a man on the edge of

the grave, but his previous words, "Thine eyes shall
be upon me, but I shall not be" (7:8), gave no indica-
tion that he had an *assured* hope of life beyond the
tomb. The "land of the shadow of death" is apparently to him a "land of *thick darkness, as darkness
itself*," for he said, "He that goeth down to the grave
cometh up no more" (7:9).

Job has walked with God in this present world and
known His blessing in the things of time, but he is to
learn in his affliction what he did not know in his
prosperity; for the realities of the other world seem
only to be unveiled to us when all of this world has
been loosened from our grasp.

Job compares the frail life of man to a flower which
springs forth and is cut down as quickly (14:1–2).

"*Dost Thou*"—the Omnipotent, Eternal God—"*open
Thine eyes upon such an one?*" he cries to Jehovah. Is
it possible that Thou wilt deal severely with me—a
frail human being—and bring me unto judgment
with *Thee* (14:3), for "*who can bring a clean thing out
of an unclean?*" (14:4).

By these words we see that Job clearly recognizes
that man, *as he is in himself,* is unclean, even as
David the Psalmist wrote: "They are all gone aside;
they are together become filthy; there is none that
doeth good, no, not one" (Psalm 14:3; see also Romans 3:9–12).

That a "clean thing" cannot "come out of an unclean" is as true as that a corrupt tree cannot bring
forth good fruit. "That which is born of the flesh is
flesh," and there is no hope for fallen man but to
begin again and to be born from above.

Job understands that there is *hope for a tree* if it is
cut down; new life may spring again (14:7–9); but as
for man if *he* dies, "Where is he?" (14:10). He passes
away "as the waters are gone from the sea" (14:11).
When he lies down to his last sleep, he will not wake

again until the heavens be no more (14:12).

If God *is* angry with me, oh that I could thus be hidden in the grave until His anger has passed away (14:13), cries Job. He wishes that the Lord would appoint a set time when He would remember him and restore His favor to him, but the thought comes, "*If a man die, shall he live again?*" (14:14). If he could only be sure of this, he would wait patiently all the days of conflict until his release should come, until he would hear the voice of God calling him to another life—when he would answer Him quickly and know that after all the Lord truly had a desire for the work of His hands (14:14–15).

But now, Job reverts to his present condition. God appears to be counting his steps and watching minutely for sin so that He might "seal" and fasten up his transgressions and iniquity, as it were, in a bag (14:16–17).

Surely water ceaselessly running *wears away even stones,* and Job is feeling quite worn out with the conflict. This prolonged trial is destroying every bit of hope (14:19). A man in such a state cannot notice anything going on around him: if his sons are honored, he does not know it; if they are brought low, he does not see it (14:21). Job is in such a condition that he senses only the pain of his *own* body and mourns only for *himself* (14:22).

CHAPTER 6

"Humble yourselves . . . under the mighty hand of God, that He may exalt you in due time." (1 Peter 5:6)

ELIPHAZ' SECOND INDICTMENT, AND JOB'S HUMILIATION

"Then answered Eliphaz, . . . Thine own mouth condemneth thee, and not I." (Job 15:1, 6)

ELIPHAZ again speaks and charges Job with doing away with the fear of God: he is diminishing "devotion" (15:4, mg.) by liberty of speech in addressing Him. The language he uses *proves his iniquity*; his tongue is crafty; his own lips testify against him; he condemns himself by his own mouth (15:5–6).

Once more Eliphaz employs the weapon of sarcasm in dealing with the stricken man. "*Art thou the first man that was born?*" Do you listen in on God's council and limit wisdom to *yourself* (15:7–8)? "*What knowest thou, that we know not? What understandest thou, which is not in us?*" he says. "With *us* are both the grayheaded and the very aged men, much older than thy father" (15:9–10)!

Eliphaz appeals to *age* as proof of wisdom. Did Job presume to think he knew more of God than these aged men. "*Us,*" said Eliphaz! This "*us*" meets us again and again in every human story. "He followeth not *us!*" cry the disciples to the Lord in after years.

"Do you presume to know more than we know?" cries Eliphaz to Job. Tradition, age, the voice of the

71

majority—all this carries weight. Will you—one man—
stand out against the united conclusions of all of *us?*
Is there any secret sin you have, Job? "*Why doth
thine heart carry thee away?*" (15:12) that "*thou turnest
thy spirit against God,*" for God is with *us!* Do the
"*consolations of God*" we are offering you seem too little
for you (15:11), even "*the word that dealeth gently
with thee*"?

Eliphaz continues that he did not think a man
could be righteous before God—a God so holy that
even the heavens were not clean in His sight (15:14–
15). And then, applying his words to Job: "*How much
less one that is abominable and corrupt, a man that
drinketh iniquity like water!*" (15:16).

This is simply an echo of the spirit-voice that
Eliphaz was relying upon as his authority for dealing
with Job, and the language proves that "visions"
given to the soul by agents of the Adversary *do not
result in deliverance from the power of sin,* whereas
the Holy Spirit reveals the truth of God for the one
purpose of freeing the sinner from his sins.

Moreover, the devil often makes use of a half-truth
to blind his captives. He is quite satisfied that Eliphaz
should believe in the utter corruption of fallen man *if
thereby he will remain in it* and continue to "*drink
iniquity like water.*"

The message of the gospel comes to fallen man and
offers to make him a *new* creature. He is bidden to
take his place in Christ upon His cross and "put off . . .
the old man, which is corrupt," and "put on the new
man . . . created in righteousness and holiness of
truth."

Taught of God, Job, offering the burnt offerings
commanded him, had learned in *experience* the way
to God, although he could not have explained it in
New Testament language. The words he uses show
that he clearly knew what he was in himself, but he

also knew in his heart that *he had access to God* and had walked before Him with the witness in his soul of integrity and truth, being kept by Jehovah Himself from all that he knew to be evil.

It was this confidence that the friends did not understand, for they measured him by their own knowledge and experience.

Eliphaz is not able to do more than *assert* that man is too corrupt and filthy to hope to stand righteous before God. He had been taught it by a spirit-vision, but he cannot explain it further, so he will keep to the line of things he does understand, to the tradition he has been taught by the fathers (15:17–19). He will describe again to Job the portion of the wicked man, the one who defies God and behaves himself proudly against El-Shaddai (15:25).

Authentic tradition, carefully preserved and handed down from the fathers, as well as his own eyesight, proved that the wicked man travailed in pain all his days (15:20); he was always in terror, he had no prosperity (15:21), no bread (15:23), no permanent home (15:28), no riches (15:29), no fruit (15:33–34), in fact nothing but distress, anguish and darkness (15:23–24) because he refused to yield to the Almighty.

Job's Reply to Eliphaz

"I have heard many such things; wearisome comforters are ye all." (Job 16:2, mg.)

"*Miserable comforters*" in truth these men were to the afflicted Job. If *you* were in my place and "*if your soul were in my soul's stead, I could join words together against you, and shake mine head at you,*" he replies to Eliphaz (16:4).

"It is so easy," cries Job, "when we are not in the

furnace ourselves, to *'talk to the grief'* [Psalm 69:26,
A.V.] of those who are suffering"!

It is true that we can only minister the comfort of
God to others so far as we ourselves have realized it
in our own lives. This was the secret of Paul's tactful
tenderness with suffering souls. He understood that
he was being fitted by his afflictions to minister to
others. "Whether we be afflicted, it is for *your* comfort
and salvation," he writes to the Corinthians, and
"whether we be comforted, it is for *your* comfort,
which worketh in the patient enduring of the same
sufferings which we also suffer" (2 Corinthians 1:6).

But, said Job to Eliphaz, if *you* had been in my
place, suffering as I am, I would have tried to
strengthen you with my mouth, *not cast you down
and condemn you*; I would have sought to assuage
your grief with consoling speech (16:5) instead of
callous reasonings and philosophizings over the
greatness of God and the corruption of man, and
telling me I was only being given what I deserved!

Alas, what "miserable comforters" we children of
God ofttimes are! Though we live in the full light of
the gospel and in the knowledge of Him who was
made "perfect through sufferings," many of us still
have hidden in our hearts the very same thoughts as
those of the friends of Job and are disposed to make
freedom from suffering a test—*for others* and *ourselves*—of being "right with God." "Christ bore our
sorrows," we say. "He took the cross that we might be
free from a cross." How little do we understand the
deepest purposes of God in the stupendous sacrifice
of His Son upon the cross of Calvary.

Christ bore our sorrows, it is true, but it was *that
we might enter into His sorrows* over the world and
His people. He took the cross *to bring us into fellowship with Him in the cross,* and He gives us deliverance from our own burdens so that we might be free

to share *His burden of souls,* and, in our measure, fill up the afflictions of Christ for His body's sake, the Church.

For this we need to be *broken down on every side* so that we might lose the hardness that is ours in dealing with our fellow-men.

Job's Faith in God

"He hath made me weary: Thou hast made desolate all my company. And Thou hast laid fast hold on me." (Job 16:7-8)

After this complaint of the hard dealings of his friends, Job goes on to repeat that he knows he is in the hand of God.

Though I speak or not, it is all the same, he says. I am not eased (16:6). *He* has made me weary, yea, it is even God who has allowed my friends thus to deal with me and leave me desolate and without human sympathy (16:7). In my hour of trial *"mine adversary sharpeneth his eyes upon me"* (16:9). Job clearly means the Adversary *at work through human instruments,* for he goes on to say, *"They* have smitten me . . . ; *they* gather themselves together against me" (16:10).

Keenly the Adversary fixes his eye upon the soul in the furnace of trial, even "sharpening the eyes" of others to watch for the halting (i.e., faltering) of their fellows in the fire of God's crucible.

It was so with Jeremiah the prophet. He cries, "I have heard the defaming of many, terror on every side. Denounce, and we will denounce him, say all my familiar friends, they that *watch* for my halting" (Jeremiah 20:10).

No faithful servant of God has ever yet escaped this aspect of the fiery trial. "All day long they wrest my words," said David, the sweet Psalmist of Israel. Even thus are we taught fellowship with the Christ, the

Man of sorrows, and are made conformable to the image of the Lamb.

"*God hath delivered me to the ungodly,* and turned me over into the hands of the wicked" (16:11, A.V.), Job cries. "*I was at ease, and He brake me asunder; yea, He hath taken me by the neck, and dashed me to pieces; He hath also set me up for His mark*" (16:12); His archers compass me; He cleaveth my heart and doth not spare me (16:13). I cried, "*Let Him not spare,*" and He has taken me at my word. "*He breaketh me with breach upon breach; He runneth upon me*" with His power "*like a giant*" (16:14).

Job's Humiliation

"I have sewed sackcloth upon my skin, and have laid my horn in the dust." (Job 16:15)

"I have humbled myself before Him," Job continues to say; "I have covered myself with sackcloth, and laid my horn—the symbol of authority and dignity—in the dust. I have wept before Him until my face is foul (16:16) and my eyelids are swollen as under the shadow of death, although there is no violence in mine hands (16:17), and my prayer is pure."

"*Even now, behold, my witness is in heaven, and He that voucheth for me is on high*" (16:19).

It was this persistent clinging to the fact that God knew his life and God would vouch that he walked with Him in integrity of heart that aroused the indignation of the three friends of Job.

Yet what else could Job say? He knew that his prayer was sincere and pure in its motive even when *they* said it was mockery and craftiness! He knew that he had the witness of God in his soul, even though his friends scorned him (16:20) and condemned him as a willful, presumptuous man.

Job's Cessation from Struggling

"My spirit is spent. . . ." (Job 17:1, mg.)

Job turns away from his friends and reminds himself that it cannot matter much what they think: his *"spirit is spent"* with all the conflict, his days are almost over, the grave is ready for him. It was mockery to continue discussing the matter; his friends could not give him support (17:3). He must rest upon God as the First Cause. It was He who had "hid their heart from understanding" (17:4) his position. The loss was theirs, for God would not exalt them after they had denounced a friend for their own gain, even the gain of being considered right in their condemnation of Job.

After all, Job ponders, it is better that they should say what they think rather than deceive him by flattery (17:5, A.V.). It is *God* who has permitted all this and allowed him, a man who has walked in fellowship with Him, to become an open abhorring—*"one in whose face they spit"* (17:6, mg.); although by reason of the pain and sorrow of it, his eye is becoming dim and his body wasting to a shadow (17:7).

Nevertheless, the "righteous" can "hold to his ways." Though his body grows weaker, if his hands are clean and his conscience clear before God, his inner man will wax stronger and stronger (17:9).

Friends, ye can go your way, cries Job. *"I find not a wise man among you"* (17:10, mg.)! Let me be with God. *"My days are past, my purposes are broken off, even the possessions of my heart"* (17:11, mg.). There is nought before me but the grave; I have made my bed in the darkness (17:13, A.V.); I acknowledge corruption to be my native condition; it is "my father," and I have said "to the worm, Thou art my mother, and my sister" (17:14)! *"There is rest in the dust"* (17:16)!

We watch Job slowly ceasing from struggling and coming to the place of rest. So long as we writhe in our afflictions so long do we prolong them. God would have us "make our bed in the darkness," that is, *lie down in the dark* and rest in His faithfulness.

Oh soul in the hand of God, take your place in the *dust* and acknowledge that you are a sinner by nature.

Your God is watching you in the deep darkness where He has brought you; so lie down and be still. Oh soul who worships the Lord and yet walks in darkness, keep trusting in your God. Do not seek to kindle a fire by your own efforts, but wait—and you will be blest with "blessings of the *deep* that coucheth beneath," blessings that shall prevail "unto the utmost bound of the everlasting hills."

CHAPTER 7

"I saw Him . . . and He [said], Fear not: I am . . . the Living One." (Revelation 1:17-18)

BILDAD'S SECOND APPEAL, AND JOB'S PROPHETIC VISION

"Then answered Bildad, . . . Wherefore are we counted as beasts?" (Job 18:1, 3)

B ILDAD once more attempts to reason with the obstinate Job and is evidently a little hurt at Job's vigorous language in reply to Zophar.

Bildad thinks it is unkind of Job to compare his friends to the beasts and count them unclean, calling them his enemies and ungodly, and rebukes him for tearing himself apart with anger (18:4). Like a rock that cannot be moved out of its place, the fact of judgment upon the wicked could not be denied. *"The light of the wicked shall be put out"* (18:5), repeats the gentle Bildad, hardly realizing in his own heart what he is talking about.

Once more will Bildad describe for the afflicted Job the fate of the ungodly, and once more are his illustrations drawn from a very limited sphere. The light shall be put out in the tent of the wicked man (18:6); a net shall ensnare him (18:8); a gin and a snare shall lay hold of him; a noose and a trap are hidden for him (18:9-10). He shall walk in terror and be hunger-bitten (18:11-12); his family shall suffer with him (18:13); he shall be torn from the security of his tent, and brimstone shall be scattered upon his habitation (18:14–15). He shall be forgotten and have no "name" or influential position among his fellows (18:17); he shall be chased out of the world and leave no posterity (18:18–19).

In short, all who hear of him shall be shocked at his life, just as those who lived with him were horror-stricken at his fate (18:20).

The narrow scope of Bildad's mind and his smallness of heart are strikingly seen in all this. His one idea of blessing from God is prosperity in his "tent," his family, his own personal circle, and in having a "name" in the "street" in which he lived!

It was inevitable that Job should be misunderstood by such a man. How could he comprehend the depth of surrender to God shown by Job? Even more, how could he understand God's deepest purposes for His devoted servant in placing him in the crucible?

Job's Reply to Bildad

"How long, how long, Bildad, wilt thou vex my soul," cries the suffering Job, for he perceives that all these descriptions of the fate of the wicked are directed against himself. He wonders that his friends are not ashamed to deal so severely with him (19:2–3). "*Be it indeed that I have erred,*" he exclaims, I alone am responsible, "*mine error remaineth with myself*" (19:4)! His friends had no right to "magnify" themselves against him and to take a position of authority and reproach him (19:5); but in deference to Bildad's evident hurt at being counted unable to help him, he would once more describe his case and let his would-be comforters see whether they were dealing kindly with him.

Bildad had talked about the wicked being cast into a net by his *own* doings, but "Know now," Job solemnly says, "*God hath overthrown me,* and hath compassed me with *His net*" (19:6, mg.). *God* had brought him into a position where he could not move one way or another; he was cast into a net thrown around him by *God Himself.*

Job's friends had bidden him set his heart aright and stretch out his hands to God, but he *had* cried out and was not heard (19:7). He knew, however, that it was *God* who was dealing with him; it was He who had fenced up his way and set darkness in his paths (19:8) so that he could not see one step before him; it was *God* who had stripped him, taken the crown from his head, and broken him down on every side so that even hope seemed gone, "*plucked up like a tree*" (19:9–10). It was *God* who had severed him from his brethren and his acquaintances and left him to suffer his sorrows alone (19:13).

"*My kinsfolk have failed,*" cries the lonely man. "*My familiar friends have forgotten me*"—they who were glad to know me in the day of prosperity, they who have eaten my bread and sojourned with me, now "*count me for a stranger*" (19:14–15).

My servants also treat me as a stranger; when I call, they do not answer; I have to entreat where once I commanded (19:16). I am repulsive to my wife and loathsome to my relatives; "*even young children despise me; if I arise, they speak against me*" (19:17–18).

Keenest pain of all, the "*men of my council*" (19:19, mg.), "*my inward friends,*" the ones who knew me intimately and those who I thought would cling to me and believe in me whatever came, even they who I tenderly loved "*are turned against me*" (19:19)! Could any man be in a more desolate state?

What have I left? Look at me, friends, bereft of all, see—"*my bone cleaveth to my skin*"—I am escaped out of all this calamity with but the "*skin of my teeth*" (19:20). "*Have pity upon me, have pity upon me, O ye my friends: for the hand of God hath touched me"* (19:21).

The hand of God! Job little knew of the scene that had taken place in heaven. *"Put forth Thine hand now, and touch all that he hath; . . . touch his bone and his flesh, and he will renounce Thee,"* Satan had said to Jehovah.

God had done it—or, more correctly, had permitted His faithful servant to be tried by the Adversary—and there is no sign yet of Job's renunciation of God. True, he had wept, groaned and writhed under his sufferings, but the loyalty of his soul had never been shaken. *To him all had come from the "hand of God."* He could not understand why the Lord should thus deal with him: *why* He appeared to be judging him; but he knew that his conscience was clear and that pity and sympathy should have been given him by his friends.

Job's Prophetic Vision

> "But I know that my Redeemer liveth, and that He shall stand at the latter day upon the earth; and after I shall awake, though this body be destroyed, yet out of my flesh shall I see God." (Job 19:25-26, mg.)

On the dung-heap see the once honored chief, apparently forsaken by God and man, a loathsome wreck of skin and bone.

Being persecuted, he endures; being defamed, he entreats; made as filth of the world and the off-scouring of all things, in his hour of deepest degradation and shame he breaks out into a burst of triumphant faith that, even though his body be destroyed, he has the glorious assurance that he shall yet see God!

Job's spirit is suddenly set free and breaks out into the light. His "Vindicator" (19:25, mg.) is living! At the latter day He shall stand upon the earth. "What does it matter if worms do destroy this body, I shall yet see God," cries Job. "*See Him for myself,*" and "*on my side.*" Mine eyes shall behold Him, and He will not be a stranger. How my inner being is consumed with earnest desire for that day (19:27, mg.).

Job had said not long before this, "Shall a man live again?" and his question *has been answered through his own lips.* He has not only been given a glimpse into things to come for his own heart's comfort, but, "moved by the Holy Ghost," he has prophesied of the resurrection and coming again in glory of the crucified Redeemer.

The Apostle Paul more than once speaks of the gospel as a "*purpose of the ages*" (Ephesians 3:11, mg.), "*kept in silence through times eternal*" (Romans 16:25), "*foreordained before the worlds*" (1 Corinthians 2:7), and at last "manifested by the appearing of our Saviour Christ Jesus, who . . . brought life and incorruption to light through the gospel" (2 Timothy 1:10).

The silence has now and again been broken by some brief word from the lips of a man walking in close fellowship with God; for holy prophets "have been since the world began."

It is written that the gospel was preached beforehand to Abraham. It was also revealed by the Spirit to Job, not in the full light vouchsafed to the Apostle Paul but clearly enough for Job's own fellowship with God.

It appears also that these old-time prophets were taught the things of God *mainly by experience.*

Job might not have been able to explain the full meaning of sacrifice as the ground of access to God, but he knew the effect of it in his life; and now in the furnace of trial as he is brought to extremity, he learns *experientially the faith of the resurrection.*

Abraham was given the same knowledge in his

supreme trial, for he offered up Isaac, "*accounting that God is able to raise up, even from the dead.*"

It was the same God-given faith that enabled weak women to endure being beaten to death, not accepting deliverance, "*that they might obtain a better resurrection.*"

Such a faith the Lord sought to awaken in Martha at the tomb of her brother, and Paul the Apostle learned it in fuller measure when stoned and despairing of life in his great "trouble in Asia" (2 Corinthians 1:8–10).

Thus all through the ages we may trace the faith of the resurrection given to the soul in its moment of supreme surrender and sacrifice to God, for it appears that the hour of deepest anguish and suffering is the time when the spirit is freed to break through into a realm of light and knowledge of God never possible before.

It was so with Job. In a crucible of unparalleled suffering, brought down as he says to the "skin of his teeth," he cries, "*I know that my Redeemer liveth.*" His soul is filled with consuming desire for that glorious day when he will see his Redeemer face to face. He will be his Friend and not a stranger. He will stand upon the earth as Judge—let the friends remember this, "*there is a judgment*"—and they will have to give account to God for their hardness to Job, and "*wrathful are the punishments of the sword*" (19:28–29, mg.).

CHAPTER 8

"The Lord, whose fire is in Zion, and His furnace in Jerusalem." (Isaiah 31:9)

ZOPHAR'S INTERRUPTION, AND JOB'S REPLY

"Then answered Zophar, . . . My thoughts give answer . . . and by reason of this my haste is within me." (Job 20:1–2, mg.)

AS Job confidently speaks of a Living Redeemer, who will be his Vindicator in the day when He comes to judge the world, Zophar breaks out in haste with his reply, for he feels indignant with Job and cannot wait for him to finish what he is saying.

Zophar replies that he has heard Job's reproof putting him to shame, and his thoughts come so rapidly into his mind that he must speak (20:2–3). Job, *"Knowest thou not . . . that the triumphing of the wicked is short, and the joy of the godless but for a moment?"* (20:5).

Zophar has noticed the triumphant tone in Job's voice as, in the depths of suffering, the heavenly light breaks upon his soul. Is it really possible that Zophar thinks it but a passing emotion or the *transient exultation of a godless man?*

Bildad had called the anguished pleading of Job the "tearing" of himself with "anger," and now Zophar thinks the exultation of his spirit to be the emotional joy of the godless! Zophar said he was speaking out of his "understanding" (20:3), or, as we would say, he

was using his common sense! If Job were suffering
for some hidden sin, then it was folly to ignore the
truth and to talk of seeing God at some future time!

We say of those who are unpractical in facing the
facts of life that they "live with their heads in the
clouds," and Zophar seems to make this same charge
against Job when he says the godless man may
"*mount up to the heavens, and his head reach unto
the clouds; yet he shall perish for ever*" (20:6–7). Had
he always thought Job to be a "visionary" in religious
matters?

There is no need to follow Zophar very carefully in
the picture he presents once more to Job of the
"portion of the wicked man," the "heritage appointed
unto him by God." It is a wearisome harping upon
the same theme introduced by Bildad (Job 8:13),
continued by Eliphaz, and now taken up again by
Zophar.

It is sufficient to notice that Zophar's main idea is
that the wicked *must have their portion*—suffer their
fate—in this present world (20:29). The godless will
be chased away like a vision of the night (20:8); his
children will be oppressed (20:10, mg.); he might
obtain wealth but he shall soon lose it all (20:15); he
will keep nothing that he rejoiced in (20:20); his
prosperity will not endure (20:21); every man's hand
shall be against him (20:22); terrors will be upon him
(20:25); a fire not kindled by man will devour him
(20:26); the very heavens will reveal his sin and the
earth rise up against him (20:27).

Job's Reply

"Job answered, . . . Suffer me, and I also will speak."
(Job 21:1, 3)

The keenness of Job's anguish has evidently subsided. The tossing is over. In the faith of the resur-

rection his spirit has passed beyond the reach of his well-intentioned friends. The courtesy and restraint belonging to a man who walks in fellowship with God once more appears. He had writhed and tossed under the accusations of Zophar, but calm had returned from the moment he remembered that God was permitting his friends thus to deal with him (Job 19:13). Since his Vindicator was on high, a Living Redeemer, he would leave his case with Him. For the remainder of the discussion he treats his visitors with marked courtesy and quiet dignity, and he does not again beseech their pity or ask them to leave him. They had come with the intention of helping him, and as long as they wish to remain he will talk with them.

How foolish I have been—Job possibly thought within himself—*why* did I reason with these friends of mine? I saw from the beginning *that they did not understand.* Oh that I had silently left my case with God. They have looked up to me in the past and believed that I so walked with God that I never could be troubled; why have I allowed their words to touch me and foolishly chafed my own spirit in seeking to *make* them understand!

Job's Picture of the Wicked

> "Wherefore do the wicked . . . wax mighty in power?"
> (Job 21:7)

"Suffer me to speak" (21:3), Job courteously replies to Zophar—the one who had been anything but courteous to him—and then he meets him on his own ground. He will ignore the personal element in Zophar's words and will discuss the subject entirely apart from himself—first saying, "*As for me, is my complaint to man? And if it were so, why should not my spirit be troubled?*" (21:4, A.V.). Job feels very

keenly that he is but a human being after all. He had
walked with God, it is true, but why should he not
feel trouble like other men?

In reply to Zophar, Job presents an entirely contrary picture of the *portion of the wicked,* showing
that their punishment is not always in this world.

The wicked live and become mighty in power (21:7);
they are not left without offspring, for their children
are established before their eyes (21:8); their houses
are in peace, and the rod of God is not upon them
(21:9, mg.); their cattle increase (21:10); their children dance and sing (21:11–12); in short, they spend
their days in prosperity and go to the grave quickly
and without much suffering (21:13), although they
have deliberately said to God, "*Depart from us; for we
desire not the knowledge of Thy ways. What is the
Almighty, that we should serve Him?*" (21:14–15).

"Ye say, *Lo, their prosperity is not in their hand,*"
Job argues, but, "*How oft is the lamp of the wicked
put out, and how oft cometh their calamity upon them?*"
(21:16–17, mg.). It is true that "*God distributeth sorrows in His anger*" and "*layeth up one's iniquity for
his children*" (21:19, mg.), for the sins of the fathers
are visited upon the children, and the consequences
of sin must be even to the third and fourth generations; but as to *outward* prosperity in the things of
this world, the wicked often "have more than heart
could wish." Shall finite man teach God how to deal
with the world, "*seeing He judgeth those that are
high*"—even the angels (21:22)?

The fact is we cannot trace the ways of God. Some
men die peacefully in the time of full strength, and
others die in bitterness of soul, never having tasted
of good at all (21:23–25). They lie down in the grave
alike, and the worm deals with them alike (21:26).
We cannot explain these things or theorize upon
them; nor can we assert, in the face of facts, that the

righteous *invariably prosper* and the wicked *invariably suffer* in this present world.

After this calm reply to Zophar, Job reverts again to his personal position. There is no heat nor tone of complaint now in his language. He simply shows his friends that he understands their aim. "*I know your thoughts and the devices which ye wrongfully imagine against me*" (21:27), he says. When you speak of the portion of the wicked, you are saying to yourselves, "*Where is the house of the prince? And where is the tent wherein the wicked dwelt?*" (21:28).

I know I have now no tent. The once mighty prince has no place but the dunghill, but do you wise men not understand that "the evil man is often spared in the day of calamity" and reserved for a *future* judgment, even the "day of wrath"? (21:30, mg.).

You would-be comforters have sought to comfort me with vain reasonings that have no foundation in fact and actual experience.

In your answers to all that I have said, there has only been *faithlessness* (21:34, mg.)—faithlessness in *God's faithfulness to His children,* and *faithlessness in the integrity of my walk with Him*; therefore you have failed to comfort me.

CHAPTER 9

"I will bring the third part through the fire, and will refine them as silver is refined, and will try them as gold is tried." (Zechariah 13:9)

ELIPHAZ' LAST APPEAL, AND JOB'S ANCHOR OF FAITH

"Then answered Eliphaz, . . . Is not thy wickedness great?" (Job 22:1, 5)

ELIPHAZ has not yet spoken his last word. One more attempt must be made to press conviction home. Since Job persistently refuses to acknowledge transgression as the cause of his affliction, he must be dealt with more definitely, and Eliphaz will put before him in detail some possible ways in which he has grieved the Lord.

The friends all through show a most lamentable ignorance of the character of God. They appear to exalt Him in their talk of His greatness and holiness, but they do not seem to have any real acquaintance with Him, although Eliphaz later on urges Job to this personal knowledge of God.

"Is it any *pleasure* to El-Shaddai that thou art righteous, or is it *gain* to Him, that thou makest thy ways perfect?" Eliphaz asks Job (22:3).

Yet it is written that "*the Lord taketh pleasure in His people.*" He "taketh pleasure in them that fear Him." How little did Eliphaz know the *heart* of God!

"Is it for thy *fear* of Him that He reproveth thee?" (22:4), he sarcastically continues. Judging by the extent of the "*reproof*," Job's wickedness must be very great. His iniquities must have been unending, since there seemed to be no end to his sufferings (22:5)!

Eliphaz' favorite weapon is *sarcasm*. His words to Job here are almost clothed with this. After listening to all that had passed, he sees it is hopeless to convince Job by flank attacks. He will cast aside all cover and speak out his mind for the last time. Job had just said that he knew they were preaching at him in their histories of the fate of the wicked, so Eliphaz would speak out.

"Job, *is not thy wickedness great?*" You are simply receiving your portion in all the suffering that has come upon you. It is a judgment for your sins, cries Eliphaz, as he goes on to enumerate these sins.

Job must have robbed his brethren, cruelly stripped the poor, withheld water from the weary and bread from the hungry (22:6-7), been deaf to the cry of the widow, and taken advantage of the fatherless (22:9); therefore snares were around him, and sudden fear troubled him. Did he not *see* that he was in darkness and deep waters (22:10-11, mg.)?

Worse than all, Job was saying in his heart that God did not know all this—that Jehovah was too high and too hidden with clouds as He walked on the vault of heaven to see what Job was doing (22:12-14, mg.).

From the pedestal of his assumed knowledge of God, Eliphaz looks pityingly down upon this poor sin-punished friend of his.

"*Dost thou mark the old way which wicked men have trodden?*" (22:15, mg.). Will you not take warning by their fate—they who said to God, "*Depart from us*"—he cries.

Eliphaz' Last Appeal

"Acquaint now thyself with Him, and be at peace: thereby good shall come unto thee." (Job 22:21)

From candid words Eliphaz turns to pleading, for he genuinely desires to help this stricken man. If Job would but *acquaint himself* with God, he would be at peace and good should come to him and not evil (22:21). He strongly urges him to receive instruction from the mouth of God and to lay up His words in his heart (22:22, mg.), for it was sad to see such havoc as appeared in Job's life through persistent refusal to listen to the advice of the friends now pleading with him.

If Job would only *return* to El-Shaddai, he would be built up instead of being broken down; if he would put away unrighteousness from his home and lay his treasure in the dust, El-Shaddai Himself would be his treasure (22:23–25).

Then Job would delight himself in El-Shaddai; he would lift up his face to God without the "terrors" that he speaks about (22:26); his prayers would be answered; he would be enabled to fulfill his promises to God; power and authority would be restored to him, for he could then "*decree a thing*" and it would be done. Instead of darkness, *light* would shine upon his ways (22:27–28). He would be able to say confidently to those who were cast down, "*There is lifting up*" (22:29), and he would be used once more to help and bless others. Souls would be delivered because he had put away unrighteousness, confessed his transgressions, and made clean his hands (22:29–30).

Job's Reception of Eliphaz' Appeal

"Then Job . . . said, Even today is my complaint accounted rebellion: His hand is heavier than my groaning. Oh that I knew where I might find Him." (Job 23:1–3, mg.)

Job does not reply to Eliphaz at once; for the assumption that he is a transgressor and the unrelenting accusations of wrongdoing, with the renewed exhortation to put away sin and seek God, are more than he can answer. The iron is entering his soul, and he can only pour out his heart to God.

"Even today is my complaint bitter," Job groans in his anguish. Oh if he could but get access to the throne of God, he would spread out his case before Him; if he could but get *His* verdict and understand *His* will, he would be satisfied (23:3–5). If he could but come even to the seat of Jehovah, he is sure that the Lord would not contend with him in the greatness of His power. He would give heed to His servant (23:6) and permit him to reason with Him so that he might be delivered from all the cruel judgment of his friends (23:7).

The Test of Faith

> "Behold, I go forward, but He is not there; and backward, but I cannot perceive Him: He worketh on the left hand, but I cannot behold Him: He hideth Himself on the right hand, that I cannot see Him." (Job 23:8–9)

Job is obliged to confess that he has no word from God in his deep trial. Whichever way he moves— forward, backward, to the left or to the right—he cannot perceive a trace of His presence or His workings.

This hiding of God gives the bitterest pain of all, but it is useless laboring to find Him when He withdraws Himself from the consciousness; no agonizing in prayer or writhing in self-effort can compel Him to unveil His face when He hides Himself in thick darkness.

Whatever Eliphaz may think about it, even though he calls Job's complaint *rebellion,* yet Job is bound to acknowledge his position. *Jehovah has broken him down on every side,* and there is no possibility of "keeping up appearances" now. God has hidden Himself from him, and he does not know why!

The Anchor of Faith

> "*But* He knoweth the way that I take; when He hath tried me, I shall come forth as gold." (Job 23:10)

But if I cannot see God, He can see me, cries Job. If I do not know the path He is leading me in, *He* knows it and that is enough. *He* has placed me in the crucible of trial; and when the fire has done its work, He will bring me forth as gold (23:10).

In spite of all Job's suffering and his outpouring of bitter complaint, writhing as he was under the endurance of what was almost unendurable to a human being, we cannot but see again and again how Job was really made to understand his position by the inner teaching of the Spirit of God. We may continually discern the difference between the inner and the outer man through the language he uses.

As we listen to his outpourings of grief, it seems as if at times the inner man was lost in the bitter cries of the outward man which was perishing day by day; yet again and again the *inner spirit* breaks forth in the tenacity of the faith which assured him, in the face of outward seemings, that he is still in the hand of God.

Again we see that at the moment of deepest despair when Job is driven to an agonized cry to his friends for pity, his spirit breaks free in triumphant faith in the living God. He is anchored afresh upon the Rock, so that now—when Eliphaz boldly deals with him as a transgressor and he is dumb with the manifest impossibility of answering him—he is able to steadfastly rest in the faithfulness of God and to understand what El-Shaddai is doing with him.

Job remembers that *gold must always be purified by fire*. He had learned in days gone by the efficacy of sacrifices for the remission of sins, but now he knows that there is a trial by fire for the gold of God's elect, and true gold will stand the fire and only lose the dross which must be purged away.

Job had writhed under the charges of evildoing and bitterly cried to God to show him his transgressions; but from the moment he had seen his Redeemer to be his heavenly Vindicator, his spirit rests in calm assurance and dependence upon God. He knew now that Jehovah was only *trying* him, not punishing him as his friends had said.

The Boldness of Faith

> "My foot hath held fast to His steps; His ways have I kept, and turned not aside. I have not gone back. . . ."
> (Job 23:11–12)

"Beloved, if our heart condemn us not we have boldness toward God," is the New Testament explanation of these bold words from Job.

Job knew that he had not swerved from his fixity of purpose to walk in the ways of God. He declared that his foot had held fast to His steps; that is, that the foot of faith had been planted firmly upon every fresh step onwards, for Jehovah the Lord had been his strength, making his feet like deer's feet to walk upon the high places of His truth.

Moreover, Job could say with a clear conscience that he had not "turned aside" or "gone back" from anything that he knew to be the will of God: he had *"treasured up the words of His mouth"* and esteemed them more than his *"necessary food"* (23:12).

Hence we have the secret of Job's fear of the Lord and dread of sin. He knew what it was to receive *"words from His mouth."* Such words remain in the heart as letters of fire, cannot be effaced, and are of far more value to spirit, soul and body than even necessary food.

The Lord Christ knew this when He said to the tempter urging Him to provide for His own bodily needs, "Man shall not live by bread alone, but by *every word that proceedeth out of the mouth of God.*"

Does this mean also the written word as we have it in the Scriptures? Yes, for when *the Holy Spirit of God speaks through the Scriptures,* every word is given to the soul as if freshly out of the mouth of God. Furthermore, we are plainly told that the *letter* killeth; it is the Spirit alone, speaking through the letter, who giveth life.

The Knowledge of Faith

> "But He is in one mind, and who can turn Him? and what His soul desireth, even that He doeth. For He performeth that which is appointed for me: and many such things are with Him." (Job 23:13–14)

Job's knowledge of the character of God comes out very clearly again and again. Here he shows that he knows Him as the Changeless One, with whom there "can be no variation, neither shadow that is cast by turning" (James 1:17).

The immutable God could not be hindered or turned aside from fulfilling His purposes. Job could rest assured that Jehovah would perform all the desires of His heart for him. *"And many such things are with Him,"* Job adds. Many blessed purposes are in His heart for me, and He will take His own way to fulfilling them. I only know that *"What His soul desireth, even that He doeth"*; none can turn Him aside.

Oh blessed rest in God, the Immutable One! Job has truly anchored within the veil ever since his

spirit fled for refuge to God and he was given the
assurance of a Living Redeemer who would vindicate
him in the day of His appearing.

The Fear of Faith

"Therefore am I troubled at His presence; when I
consider, I am afraid of Him. For God maketh my heart
soft and the Almighty troubleth me." (Job 23:15–16,
A.V.).

These seem strange words to follow the bold language that Job has just used, but in experience they
are easily understood.

The outward man had been broken down on every
side, and in the breaking all natural power of endurance and self-restraint had gone. The once dignified
Job had not been able to hide his sufferings behind a
barrier of reserve, nor had he been able to protect
himself from the humiliation of pleading for pity from
his misjudging friends.

He knew that God was refining him as gold, and he
understood that He was only performing for Him the
deep purposes of His heart for eternal blessing. But
he remembered the wormwood and the gall of the
past days as he said the words, *Many such things
are with Him,* and he could not help trembling as to
what those "many things" might mean in further
suffering.

Job says, "When I consider, I am *afraid* of Him,"
and he explains this by adding, *"God maketh my
heart soft,"* even though "I am not dismayed because
of the darkness, nor because thick darkness covereth
my face" (23:17, mg.).

Job does not know how the fire is doing its work in
him. But a soft or melted heart can *only* be obtained
by *fire*!

"Yea, I will gather you, and blow upon you with the

fire . . . and ye shall be melted . . ." (Ezekiel 22:21) was the Lord's message to Israel in later years, and Isaiah says the manifested presence of God is as the *"fire of meltings"* to His people.

A soft heart has lost resistance to the hand of God not only in *will—*for *the will may have been unresisting long before—*but in regard to an *involuntary* hardness that makes its capacity small and narrow.

"Be ye enlarged," writes the Apostle Paul to the Corinthians, and the heart can only be enlarged when it is softened and melted by the fire.

Job is conscious of the softened heart that melts within him at the presence of God, but he knows too that its cause is not *fear—*fear of the thick darkness that God is leading him through. He does not know what the reason is, but his heart is faint.

The Marvel of Faith

> "Why is it, seeing times are not hidden from El-Shaddai, that they who know Him see not His days?" (Job 24:1, mg.)

How is it, if my friends know God, ponders Job, that they do not *understand His different times* or "days" for dealing with souls?

For instance, there are some people so selfish and grasping that they provide for their own needs regardless of the suffering of others, take advantage of the fatherless, rob the widow, trample on the poor, so that all are afraid of them (24:2–4). Then there are the poor who are oppressed: they work hard for daily food, they reap the grain and glean the vintage, yet they are without shelter at night and have no covering from the cold (24:5–8).

The oppressor robs the fatherless and the poor (24:9); and the oppressed for the sake of food work within the walls of these men (24:10–11); and out of the populous city are heard the groans and the cries of these oppressed souls (24:12). Yet God does not deal with either, for it is not His "day" or time for doing so.

Then again there is the murderer, the thief, the adulterer, all who sin in the dark and hide themselves in the daytime (24:14–17). "*Ye say . . . their portion is cursed in the earth*" (24:18, mg.) and that "the grave" violently takes away all who thus sin (24:19, mg.); but the fact is "*God giveth them to be in security*" (24:23) because it is not yet the "day" for dealing with them.

It is true His eyes are upon their ways: in a little while they are gone; and when they are brought low, they are gathered in and cut off like ears of grain (24:23–24).

Am I not speaking truth, Eliphaz? God has a time for *all* things, and those who know Him should see and understand His "days" (24:25).

CHAPTER 10

"I counsel thee to buy of Me gold refined by fire, that thou mayest become rich." (Revelation 3:18)

BILDAD'S LAST WORD, AND JOB'S REPLY

"Bildad the Shuhite said, . . . *How* . . . *?*" (Job 25:1–6)

BILDAD has yet a few words to say, but they do not seem very appropriate at this stage. He ignores all that has passed between Job and his other friends and harks back to the question propounded by the spirit-voice to Eliphaz, which Job dealt with in answer to Bildad's first pleading.

The question as to *how* a man could be just before God is still upon Bildad's mind. He replies to Job that God is the One who certainly has complete dominion, for He is the Lord of Hosts; there is no numbering of His armies and His light shines upon all men, both good and evil (25:2–3). But the question remains to be answered: Since Jehovah is so great and mighty, *how* then can man be *just* before Him? "*How* can he be clean" when even "*the stars are not pure in His sight: how much less man, that is a worm?*" (25:4–6, mg.).

Job's Reproach of Bildad

"Job . . . said, *How* hast thou helped him that is without power? *How* hast thou saved [him without] strength? *How* hast thou counselled him that hath no wisdom? . . . And whose spirit came forth from thee?" (Job 26:1–4)

101

Job answers Bildad's "How?" with some other "Hows?" more to the point than the question which was occupying his thoughts.

If Bildad did not know how to find acceptance with God and how to have a clear conscience before Him, what right had he to come with his *negations* to a man in affliction? All his utterances had been about the *calamities* which would come upon those who forgot God.

Job asks Bildad plainly what sort of help *he* had given to one without power and what kind of salvation *he* had to offer to one who had no strength to save himself (26:2). What *counsel* had he for one in perplexity and darkness? Had he "*plentifully declared sound knowledge*" to the one he had come to teach (26:3), and what *spirit* had come forth from him to encourage and help his friend in the time of trouble (26:4)?

Bildad's "How?" is best answered by reminding him of the omnipotence of God. All things visible and invisible are open to Him. The "shades" beneath the waters tremble; the "grave" is naked, and "destruction" has no covering before Him (26:5–6, mg.). He made the earth and hung it over nothing, upholding it by the word of His power (26:7); He covers the face of the full moon when He pleases, and none can see it through the clouds that surround it (26:9, mg.); He controls the mighty waters; the pillars of heaven tremble before Him; He stills the sea and smites arrogancy (26:10–12); and by His Spirit He makes the heavens beautiful, His hand piercing even the gliding serpent (26:13, mg.).

All these are but the "outskirts," the outer fringe "of His ways" (26:14), and in all these mighty workings" how "small a whisper" do we hear of Him. How silently and quietly He works! If we cannot trace the edges of His ways, much less can we understand the "thunder" or full manifestation of His mighty deeds (26:14, mg.).

Bildad's "How?" is *answered by the power of God.* If He works all these wondrous things in the world of nature, is it possible that His noblest work of creation—man—is beyond His power? It is true that compared with his Creator man is but a *worm* and has fallen from his first estate to become the slave of the world he was created to rule over, but God is able to devise means whereby His banished may be restored to Him.

Job cannot answer Bildad's question beyond again reminding him of the omnipotence of God.

Job's Integrity

> "Job again took up his parable, and said, As God liveth, . . . till I die I will not put away mine integrity. . . ." (Job 27:1–5)

Job appears to have been interrupted by the interjection of Bildad's question.

Job had been saying (Job 23) how God was performing all things for him and had then lapsed into meditation over the strange ignorance of God's "times" or "ways" shown by those who professed to know Him. After replying to Bildad (Job 26), he resumes the thread of his "parable," or narrative, and solemnly closes it with a deliberate and final affirmation that he intends to hold fast to his integrity to the very end.

"*As the Lord of Hosts liveth, before whom I stand,*" was the language of Elijah when bearing fearless testimony to Israel.

"*As God liveth,*" said Job with the same consciousness of standing before Him in integrity of heart and life. The Spirit of God is in me, he continues to say. "*Surely my lips shall not speak unrighteousness*" nor utter deceit (27:3–4). In His presence I cannot justify you, my friends, nor say that you have dealt rightly with me. Neither can I go back from what I know before God to be my true attitude of soul. I cannot say that I have forsaken the ways of God when "my heart doth not reproach me for any of my days" (27:6, mg.).

"*Till I die,*" declares Job, "*I will not put away mine integrity from me.*" I have walked with God in righteousness and truth. I hold fast to this confidence in spite of all my strange afflictions, and I "*will not let it go*" (27:5–6).

Those who "rise up against me" and falsely condemn me when I am innocent of their charges are not friends but enemies, and upon *them* will come the "portion of the wicked" (27:7).

Job asks what he would gain by being a hypocrite. In his time of need would God hear his cry (27:8–9)? A hypocrite would not have called upon God "at all times" and delighted himself in the Almighty as he had done (27:10).

Job's Teaching of His Teachers

"I will teach you concerning the hand of God." (Job 27:11)

It was Zophar's turn to speak after Bildad's last brief speech, but Zophar is silent—whereupon Job breaks out with the words, "*I will teach you concerning the hand of God; that which is with the Almighty will I not conceal.*" He will show his would-be teachers that he is not blind; for he had seen the other aspect of the "portion of the wicked" in this world as well as they, and he could describe their sorrows as well as their prosperity. Why were his friends so vain as to think that none had eyes to see except themselves (27:12)? He would not "conceal" or keep back what he knew concerning the hand of God.

It was *not* true that *suffering was invariably the fruit of sin,* but it was true—terribly true—that a life of utter disregard of God and sinful self-grasping must have sore consequences in this world and the next.

It *was* true that if in some cases the children of the oppressor were multiplied, it was for the sword; those children would never be content with simple necessary food, for they would be possessed by the restless, dissatisfied spirit they had seen in their home (27:14); the *oppressor* would have no lamentation made over him at his death, for his true character would come out at the last and repel even those who had loved him (27:15); he might heap up silver and personal possessions, but he would have to leave it all at the end (27:16–17); he might build his house with great trouble as the spider weaves his web, but it would prove to be but a temporary shelter after all (27:18); he might lie down rich, but his riches would not save him, for he would be swept away as by a sudden tempest or an east wind blighting his life (27:19–21). In short, God would lay His hand upon him suddenly and say, "*Thou foolish one, this night is thy soul required of thee,*" and he would desperately try to get out of God's hand, but it could not be (27:22). Men would also accord with Jehovah's dealing and "*hiss him out of his place*" with no regret (27:23).

This would be the *end* of the ungodly, even though the rod of God had not been visibly upon him and his household in earlier years.

The Heavenly Wisdom Described

"Surely there is mine for silver, and a place for gold which they refine." (Job 28:1)

After Job has described the "heritage of oppressors" and shown the folly of those who set their hearts upon the things of time, he breaks out into a striking description of the trouble and pain with which men seek for earthly treasure and contrasts the wisdom enabling them to obtain the riches hidden in the earth with the value of the wisdom which comes from above.

Precious silver has to be dug with much labor out of a mine; gold must needs be placed in a furnace to be refined; iron has to be taken out of the dust in which it lies, and copper has to be melted out of stone (28:1-2, mg.).

With what perseverance men explore the darkest depths of the earth for the precious metals, searching the furthest recesses (28:3) and breaking open shafts into the earth, far away from the dwellings of men, so that they might obtain the treasures it contains (28:4).

Yea, even out of the dark earth comes food for the sustenance of man, and from its very stones, beautiful gems that glow like fire, sapphires of transparent blue and dust of gold (28:5-6).

The path of the miner into the bowels of the earth searching for concealed treasure cannot be traced by the keenest sighted "bird of prey." Nor can the proud beast that roams on the surface—not even the fierce lion—tread this path after the foot of man (28:7-8), as he removes the flinty rock, overturns mountains by the roots, cuts out passages among the rocks, his eye searching for "every precious thing" (28:9-10), and diverting streams of water so that the hidden treasures might be brought to light (28:11).

Such is the eagerness with which men seek for earthly riches. They understand the value of gold, but *do they know the greater value of true wisdom and knowledge* (28:12-13)?

If they *do* set their hearts upon getting it, do they know where to *find* it? It is not in the depth of the earth nor in the sea (28:14). No gold or silver can buy it; even precious stones and the gold of Ophir cannot be compared with it (28:15–16). Its value is *above* all the precious things of earth, and it cannot be obtained even for vessels of pure gold (28:17, mg.). "Yea, *the price of wisdom is above rubies*" (28:18).

"*Whence then cometh wisdom?*" seeing that it cannot be found on earth, nor purchased by the most precious things of earth, and is "hidden from the eyes of all living" (28:20–21)?

"*God understandeth*" the source of wisdom and alone can teach the way of obtaining it. *All wisdom is hidden in God Himself.* "He looketh to the ends of the earth, and *seeth under the whole heaven*" the hidden things which men discover with great labor. "Yea, He meted out the waters by measure" and determines a "weight for the wind" (28:24–27); therefore He alone knows the place of wisdom, and *He* says:

"Behold, the fear of the Lord . . . is wisdom; and to depart from evil is understanding" (28:28).

In brief, *men* think that wisdom is *knowledge*—knowledge of gaining treasures from the bowels of the earth, knowledge of how to refine gold, to melt iron, to polish brilliant stones, to blast flinty rocks, to remove mountains by their skill, and to divert mighty rivers, so that, as it were, all the secrets hidden in the earth are under their command and control—but *God* says that the highest wisdom is to be obtained in knowing *Him*, in understanding *His* will, and in "*departing from evil.*"

This is the wisdom which "cometh from above," for "the Lord giveth wisdom; out of His mouth cometh knowledge and understanding" (Proverbs 2:6).

CHAPTER 11

"The fining pot is for silver, and the furnace for gold, and a man is tried by that which he praiseth." (Proverbs 27:21, mg.)

JOB'S STORY OF HIS PAST

"Job again took up his parable, and said, Oh that I were as in the months of old." (Job 29:1-2)

JOB now reverts to his own experience, having solemnly and finally affirmed his determination to continue in his integrity and emphatically refused to take the position urged upon him by his friends. Having silenced them, he now gives himself up to the luxury of dwelling upon the happy past while contrasting the bitterness of the present with those "months of old."

As Job takes up his "parable" and tells his story, he draws a vivid portrait of his inner and outer life as a man who walked in fellowship with God.

Unconsciously he also reveals the reason why Jehovah needed to place him in the crucible.

Job's very first words show that there was a further stage of surrender to God he had yet to learn. He had without hesitation bowed to the will of God when blow upon blow came upon him at the beginning of his great trial, but during his prolonged suffering, when emptied from vessel to vessel of pain and testing, it did not occur to him that to let his mind dwell upon past experiences and crave their return was not a full abandonment to God and an entire acceptance of His will.

A writer deeply taught in the ways of God has truly said that there has to be a very thorough surrender to the will of God for any soul in the furnace of trial never to look back with regret upon the past nor forward with any wish for the future—and yet it is easy to see that such regrets or desires are *not consistent* with a true and complete abandonment of our whole being to God.

The Adversary knows this, hence his persistent endeavor to occupy our minds with what we once were and apparently are not now, or what we *ought* to be and *seem not* to be at the moment! *Comparing ourselves with ourselves* is a fatal hindrance to present rest in the will of God.

"*O that I were as in the months of old,*" cries Job as he thinks of past experience. He says little of his former outward prosperity and the loss of property and home, however, for his heart was never centered upon the abundance of the things which he possessed. Rather, he dwells mainly upon his past fellowship with God and his life of service for others.

Job's Walk in the Light of God

> "Oh that I were . . . as in the days when God watched over me; when His lamp shined above my head, and by His light I walked through darkness." (Job 29:2–3, mg.)

Job's heart integrity is to be seen at every point of his story. In dwelling upon his past experience and his loss of all, he does not speak first even of his children, but grieves most about the cloud that has apparently come over his fellowship with God. His memory goes back to the days when he had the assurance that the Lord was watching over him, guarding and guiding every step of his life. He remembers how he walked as though a lamp were shining above or upon his head and it did not matter that deep darkness might be around him, for by the light of God he saw the path and was able to walk with Him right through the darkness.

"Oh that those blessed days were mine *again*," was the yearning longing of Job's heart. He *believed* that Jehovah was with him as formerly, but he was troubled at this new aspect of His dealings. Oh the pain of walking through darkness with no illumination upon the path, no certainty of being led by God's light through the darkness that surrounded him now.

Job was suffering as all suffer when being led by the Spirit out of the path of illumination into the walk of pure *faith* in the Faithful One. He did not know how much he had relied upon the *light* of God rather than upon God Himself; how he had walked almost by sight when the path was so illuminated, and not by faith alone.

Job knew what he had *lost*, but he did not yet realize all that he was to *gain*. His language plainly shows his position. God was watching *over* him; the lamp of God was shining *upon* him; His light shone *upon* his path. Job was to lose all this for a deeper and more intimate knowledge of God Himself, only possible to a faith that rests on the character of God alone.

Job's Friendship with God

> "Oh that I were . . . as I was in the days of my youth, when the secret [*friendship,* mg., R.V.] of God was upon my tabernacle." (Job 29:2, 4–5, A.V.)

The Revised Version text reads, "*as I was in the ripeness of my days.*" It is evident that Job regarded his *past* experience as the ripest stage of his spiritual life, but he was mistaken; later on, his vision would be clearer, and he would perceive the days of rich fruitfulness yet *before* him.

The time of youth, both in nature and in grace, is very beautiful. In the spiritual life it is lovely in fervor and freshness of love, but it has its crudities, its impulsiveness, its partiality, its assumption of knowledge, and its one-sided vision. There is beauty in fervor, devotion, energy and life, but it is the beauty of possibility, not fulfilment—the beauty of a flower that may come to ripened fruit when the petals fall.

In the days to come, Job will look back upon his past with grateful remembrance of the joy and bright light that then shone upon his path, but he will see *greater beauty in the matured faith* that walks with God in calm and quiet trust, and in the loveliness of the chastened spirit which can rest confidently in His wise and gentle workings in the world around, knowing that *all* things are being wrought after the counsel of His own blessed will.

But Job does not now see all this, for his heart is dwelling upon the past—"*when the friendship of God was upon my tent,*" he sadly says. Job did not know that Jehovah was never more his friend than now! The Lord never watched over His servant more closely than while he was in the crucible, for He does not withdraw His eyes from the fining-pot when the precious gold of His redeemed is being refined by fire.

It is now that Job refers to his children, and we see how truly he had held them for God! "*When the Almighty was yet with me, and my children were about me*" is his only mention of his family in his sad recollection of the past.

Job's Resources in God

> "My steps were washed with butter, and the rock poured me out rivers of oil!" (Job 29:6)

Job remembers what boundless resources he had had in his Almighty Friend, who smoothed all his steps for him as if they had been *"washed with butter,"* and who caused the hard rocks of difficulty in his path to pour out for him *"rivers of oil."* In fact, he had rejoiced in meeting the stumbling blocks in the road, for each one became a fresh occasion of blessing in his life.

Job's Reputation in the World

> "When I went forth . . . unto the city . . . the young men saw me and hid themselves, and the aged rose up. . . . The princes refrained talking, . . . the voice of the nobles was hushed." (Job 29:7–10)

Job's reputation as a man of God was noised abroad, and he draws a vivid picture of the way in which he was looked up to by old and young and by all classes of society.

The young feared him and *"hid themselves,"* perhaps under the impression that he would not understand or sympathize with them, or that one who lived so near to God would see them through and through—only to criticize or condemn! The aged stood up as a mark of respect, and even the princes and nobles ceased their talking when he drew near so as to listen the more readily if he had anything to say.

It is a great honor to be thus respected on account of a close walk with God. Unconsciously the reverence is really given to Jehovah. In all cases, as with Job, character carried weight, and "a man's gift [of the Holy Spirit] maketh room for him and bringeth him before great men"; but if it be that those who thus honor the servant of God "glory in men" and attach the power to the *man himself,* the Lord, who is a jealous God, must needs withdraw that soul from the eyes of others, or—as in the case of Job—place him in such a furnace of trial as to make it evident that he has nought but that which he has received from God: that *he himself* possesses no good thing!

Job's Life of Service

> "When the ear heard me, then it blessed me, . . .
> because I delivered the poor that cried, the fatherless
> also. . . . The blessing of him that was ready to perish
> came upon me: and I caused the widow's heart to sing
> for joy." (Job 29:11–13)

In striking language Job describes the joyous service for others which is the spontaneous outcome of
a life lived in close fellowship with God. When he
went forth to the city, there were those who called
down the blessing of God upon him as they heard his
voice, and every eye that saw him bore witness to the
grace and power of God upon him, and loved him for
his life of unselfish toil. This man of God was the
resort of all who were in trouble. He had the wisdom
which came from above, which is "first pure, then
peaceable, gentle, easy to be intreated, full of mercy
. . . without partiality, without hypocrisy" (James
3:17). He genuinely gave himself to the service of all
who appealed to him. The poor, the fatherless, the
person ready to perish and the widow—all found
him a ready helper, and none appealed to him in
vain.

Job's sketch of his life reaches its supremest
beauty at this point. Next to the joy of satisfying the
heart of Christ, there is no joy on earth so sweet as
that which comes from ministering to those who are
"ready to perish" and causing the lonely heart of the
widow to sing for joy.

Job looked back upon the time of privileged service
with a great longing to be entrusted with it again, but
who would come to him now—an outcast upon the
dunghill?

Job's Equipment for Service

> "I put on righteousness, and it clothed itself with
> me: my justice was as a robe and a diadem. I was eyes
> to the blind, . . . feet . . . to the lame, . . . a father to
> the needy. . . . I brake the great teeth of the unrigh-
> teous, and plucked the prey out of his teeth." (Job
> 29:14–17, mg.)

Remembering that Job's acceptance before God
was *based upon the sacrifices* he had learned to offer
to Him, we may well expect to see the same righteousness of life and character as now we find in
those who realize that the Lord Jesus Christ, "who
knew no sin, [was] made sin on our behalf, that we
might become the righteousness of God in Him" (2
Corinthians 5:21).

"*Righteousness clothed itself with me*" is the expression that Job uses to describe the force of his
life, and it shows that he was truly endued with
power from on high.

The clothing by the Holy Spirit that came upon the
disciples at Pentecost could be well described in the
same language. And did not the righteousness of
God, manifested in the power of the Spirit, clothe
itself with Peter and unveil and judge the sin of
Ananias and Sapphira?

Even so was Job an instrument in the hand of God
in his day. Clad with righteousness as a coat of mail
for the battle with sin, Job's justice—his impartial
judgment in controversy—was as a diadem of beauty
upon his head so that he was as "*eyes to the blind*" in
clearing their vision and showing them the way to
God. He was "*feet to the lame*" in strengthening them
to walk in the paths of righteousness and truth. He
was pitiful and tender with the needy, dealing with
them with a father's patience and long-suffering love,
sparing no trouble in sifting and searching out every

cause that came before him so that he might act
properly before God (29:16). He was fearless in the
battle for the right, and, regardless of consequences,
in rebuking the wicked, delivering the captives, and
plucking the wronged out of the very teeth of the
ungodly.

Job's Mistaken Confidence

"*Then* I said, I shall die in my nest; I shall multiply
my days as the sand." (Job 29:18)

Job may well have thought that he had reached the
summit of the spiritual life in the experience he
described, and which he has once before referred to
as the "ripeness of his days"!

It is thought that Job was about a hundred years
old at the time of his great trial, and no glimpses are
given of his early years; but it is clear that such
fellowship with God, such knowledge of his resources
in Him, such ripened judgment and fearless courage
in the service of others could only have been the
result of years of obedient walking before the Lord of
Hosts.

The powerful service that he describes could not
have been his time of spiritual babyhood, and yet it
was not the "ripeness of his days" as he imagines.

Job now confesses his mistaken confidence. He
had said to himself as he looked around, "*I shall die
in my nest!*" He thought he saw before him "*days
multiplied as the sand,*" for he felt his life would be
renewed like the phoenix.

He knew that his inner life was deeply rooted in
God and, as it were, opened to the living waters. The
dew of the Spirit was silently resting upon him continually and keeping him like an evergreen tree un-
touched by drought (29:19).

Moreover, his "glory" (29:20)—does he mean the continual presence of God within?—was fresh and new in him, and he was constantly being reequipped by the power of God for the conflict with sin and the powers of darkness. His "bow," instead of being weakened by use, was actually *"changed"* (mg.) and renewed while in his hand (29:20).

Job's Gift of Utterance

> "Unto me men gave ear, and waited, and kept silence for my counsel." (Job 29:21)

Job was not only clothed with the righteousness of God for the warfare with sin and the forces of darkness, but he was given in marked degree what the apostle called in Pentecostal days the "gift of utterance."

Job's description of this might have been written in the days of Paul. Envision the following abilities of the tongue manifested within a New Testament context: the *power to command a hearing* and the *intense silence* so peculiarly accompanying utterance in the Spirit (29:21); the *conviction of the Spirit* that subdues opposition and the *dew-like power* of the Spirit-given word (29:22); the *thirst* aroused and the expectancy of the hearers along with *receptivity* of heart, one's whole being opened wide as for "the latter rain" (29:23); the *faith* created by the Spirit in the God-given authority of the messenger, so that, as Job says, *"If I laughed on them, they believed it not,"* accompanied by the *light of God* that shone through the countenance of the speaker (29:24), as with Stephen before the counsel in Jerusalem.

All this cannot be said of human eloquence, and it shows that Job was truly a prophet of God in his time.

Job's Pedestal

> "I chose out their way, and sat as chief, and dwelt
> as a king in the army. . . ." (Job 29:25)

Job concludes the description of his past experience and his power in service with the significant
words: *"I . . . sat as chief"*! He compares himself to a
king in the midst of his army. There was none higher
than he! By the obedience of the people to the words
of his mouth, he practically chose out their way; and
they looked up to him and trusted him, for they knew
that they could rely upon him in every time of need.

No more solemn trust can be given to anyone than
the gift to sway hearts by speech. Such a position of
power as described by Job is perilous for any man,
and the faithful Scripture records have not hesitated
to unveil the *perils* as well as the privileges of honored servants of God.

Moses' failure with his lips, Eli's lax dealing with
his sons, David's sin through neglecting to guard his
eyes, Jeremiah's fainting of spirit in the stress of
service—all these things are written for our admonition.

The language of Job's description of his days of
spiritual power shows that he was *not indifferent to
the position in which he was placed,* both by the
manifest favor of God upon him and by the estimation of the people to whom he was sent by the Lord.

The Adversary's challenge to Jehovah had been
well timed. He had considered Job purposefully and
saw him to be in the most perilous position a human
being could occupy—one of which Paul, in later days,
knew well the danger, for he said that he had been
given a thorn in the flesh lest, through the greatness
of the revelations, he might become exalted and finally lose his crown.

On the other hand, Job's description of his experience and life strikingly confirm the words of Jehovah before the council of heaven and show that his sufferings were not the consequences of transgression or disobedience, but, by the will of God, were for the development of a *faith* which is only possible in a soul who knows the fullness of the Spirit and is being led into a walk of faith more precious to God than gold that perisheth—a faith that will be found unto *glory and honor* at the Lord's appearing.

In the New Testament, the ripened grain of wheat falling into the ground to *die* that it may bring forth much fruit, the conformity to the *death* of Christ that follows the knowledge of identification with Him on Calvary's cross, and, in Paul's personal experience, the sentence of *death* upon *all that he was in himself,* that he might rely only upon the resurrection power of God—these well correspond to this stage in Job's history.

CHAPTER 12

"Instead of His glory there shall be kindled a burning like the burning of fire. . . . And it shall be as when a standard-bearer fainteth." (Isaiah 10:16–18, mg.)

JOB IN THE CRUCIBLE

"But now . . . derision." (Job 30:1)

FROM the past with all its blessed memories, Job turns to the painful present, and the story he relates bears a strange likeness to the path of the cross trodden by the Holy Son of God when He became obedient unto death and was despised and rejected by men.

Was the history of Job not only a pattern of the ways of the Lord with His children but *also a foreshadowing of the Christ who was to come?*

Isaiah 53 was a *prophecy* depicting a suffering Messiah. Is it possible that the same portrait was dimly outlined in human story to the people of Job's day?

In any case, the inner harmony of the Scriptures is strikingly confirmed by Job's history. Externally the letter of the Word has been given "at sundry times and in divers manners," but internally we perceive the same Spirit and the same truth in unbroken unity. From Genesis to Revelation we find the reiterated message of death and resurrection, both for the Christ of God as the Representative of fallen man and for every child of Adam brought back in Him to be a child of God.

The way of the cross was trodden by the Christ in His passage from earth to heaven on behalf of His redeemed. It was the way to life abundant for Job in the ages that preceded Christ's first coming, and it is still the path of life for every soul in these latter days looking for the second appearing of the Glorified Lord.

The Path of Derision

"But now they that are younger than I have me in derision." (Job 30:1)

Job had been depicting the authority and power he had when he sat as chief and chose out the way of the people. In bitter contrast he pictures his present condition. *Then* everyone had hung upon his words. *Now* even those who were younger than he had him in derision. Not only they who were below him in age but also in position, people of a class so far beneath him that in his princely days—speaking after the manner of men—he would not have considered them fit for companionship with the dogs of his flock.

Strangely does fallen nature rejoice at the downfall of others! When a man is used by God and esteemed very highly by those who revere him for his work's sake, there are always some who look on with jealousy and envy in their hearts—even among brethren!

Can you rejoice to see another exalted even though it is at the cost of your own humiliation? Can you be genuinely glad to see your fellow-worker win a soul instead of you? See another honored and yourself humbled? Another sent forth to the service once given to you, and glory in the privilege of *hidden service* at the throne of God?

"*They that are younger than I*" was Job's complaint. Is this your cry, O servant of God, you who have borne the burden and heat of the day in the Master's service? Perhaps some young, uncultured worker, full of zeal, despises you for the apparent lack of blessing in the vineyard entrusted to your care. Are you willing to be called "old-fashioned" and to retire from the work which has been to you as your very life?

Not only do the young despise me, said Job, but gaunt and famished men (30:3–4); men who are hounded out as thieves from among others (30:5); men who are thankful to hide in the gloomiest valleys, in holes of the earth and the rocks (30:6); children of fools, base men, outcasts from the land (30:8, mg.). I am actually become the song of men like these, "*yea, I am a byword unto them*" (30:9).

The Foreshadowed Cross

"They abhor me; they . . . spare not to spit in my face; . . . upon my right hand rise the rabble; . . . as a wide breaking in of waters they come; in the midst of the ruin they roll themselves upon me." (Job 30:10–14, mg.)

From these words it appears that a crowd had gathered around the dunghill upon which Job lay, "*crucified to the world*," some hundreds of years before Christ hung upon His cross at Calvary. Such a mixed rabble gathered around the Lord. Base men were found to testify against Him, men who spoke of Him as "This fellow." He was even the song of the drunkards. Thieves were crucified with Him and assuredly had their fellows in the crowd to watch them die.

Job had spent his life in blessing the poor and needy, and now the outcasts gaze upon him, triumph in his downfall, abhor him for his repulsive condition, and spare not to spit at the sight of him.

Even so it was written of the Christ.

"All they that see Me laugh Me to scorn, they shoot out the lip, they shake the head." (Psalm 22:7).

"They have cast off all restraint" (30:11), cries Job, as he looks upon the rabble gathered around him. *"They thrust aside my feet. . . .* They set forward my calamity" (30:12–13). *"In the midst of the ruin, they roll themselves upon me"* (30:14).

Even so it was written of the Christ:

"Dogs have compassed Me: the assembly of evildoers have inclosed Me" (Psalm 22:16).

"Thou chasest my nobility as the wind" (30:15, mg.), cries Job!

"Thou knowest . . . my shame, and my dishonour" (Psalm 69:19), said the Son of God.

"My soul is poured out within me" (30:16), cries Job!

"He poured out His soul unto death" (Isaiah 53:12) was written of the Lord.

"In the night season my bones are pierced in me, and the pains . . . take no rest. . . . He hath cast me into the mire, and I am become like dust and ashes" (30:17–19), groans out stricken Job.

"They pierced My hands and My feet," and *"Thou hast brought Me to the dust of death"* (Psalm 22:15–16) was the language of the Son of God.

"I cry unto Thee, and Thou dost not answer me" (30:20) was Job's bitter complaint!

"My God, My God, why hast Thou forsaken Me? . . . O my God, I cry, . . . but Thou answerest not" (Psalm 22:1–2) was the pitiful cry of Him who was smitten of God and afflicted on our behalf.

Thus, in point after point, we may trace the story of the cross in Job's experience. Base men who were outcasts and thieves gathered around him; he was their song and their byword. They abhorred him and spat upon him. They were permitted by God to cast off all restraint in mocking him. They *cast up against him* their "ways of destruction" (30:12), charging him with their ruin because of his judgments upon them when he "plucked the prey from their teeth." The "brood" (30:12, mg.) of evildoers now had their opportunity and swept upon him as through a wide breach in the hedge that God had once placed around him. In the midst of all these awful forces of iniquity let loose upon him from without, his soul was poured out within him; his bones were pierced, and gnawing pains gave him no rest; he was disfigured and cast into the mire, brought down to dust and ashes. Above all and in all, the bitterest pang was that *God* was silent. The Lord could behold all the suffering of His servant and yet not interpose on his behalf!

As Job thinks of this unaccountable silence of the God he had served so long, he cries out with anguish in his voice, "*Thou art turned to be cruel to me*" (30:21).

Job tells the Lord that He is using the might of His hand to persecute him! He had lifted him up upon a tempest of trouble only to dissolve him in the storm (30:22), and Job was sure that He was bringing him to death, to the place appointed for all men (30:23).

Job's Collapse

> "Surely against a ruinous heap He will not put forth His hand; . . . in His destruction one may utter a cry because of these things. Did *I* not weep for him that was in trouble? . . . When *I* looked for good, then evil came." (Job 30:24–26)

"*A ruinous heap*" Job calls himself in his extremity. Then his conscience, quickly sensitive to the fear of God, smites him. What words are these that he has uttered? He had told his friends that he would trust in God even though it pleased Jehovah to slay him. He had boldly said that when his trial was finished he would come forth as gold, and now in his soul agony he charges the God he believed to be *faithful* with turning against him and persecuting him.

As the words passed his lips, Job knew that they were wrong, but he silences the still small voice within his conscience with the excuse, "One *may* utter a cry because of these things" (30:24).

Job had reached the crucial moment of his trial and did not know it. He had maintained unshaken confidence in God up to this point. The battle of words with his friends had only served to deepen his faith in God; but when he gave himself up to the luxury of dwelling upon his past, his regret and despair at his present condition grew more and more acute until he utters words of bitter reproach to his Almighty Friend.

Next came *self-excuse,* instead of quick contrition and confession of wrong accusation of his Lord; from this he sinks into *self-pity*—that he had not been given the "good" he should have had as the reward of his life of unselfish pity for others (30:25–26); then self-pity turns to *self-dejection* over his blackened condition (30:28, mg.), and finally mourning and weeping over himself in helpless and hopeless sorrow (30:29–31).

We read of a similar experience in the life of Jeremiah the prophet. Smarting under suffering caused by others, he said to the Lord, "Every one of them doth curse me. . . . I sat alone because of Thy hand; . . .wilt Thou be unto me as a deceitful brook?" *One who has failed!* And the Lord replied to the storm-tossed prophet, *"If thou takest this back, I will again let thee stand before My countenance"* (Jeremiah 15:10–19, Swedish translation).

If Job had heeded the inner warning and quickly

retracted his words to the Lord, it is probable that he would not have sunk into the wail of despair and unworthy self-vindication that followed, giving his friends the occasion for thinking that they *had been right after all* and Job *was* righteous in his own eyes.

Job's spirit has at last been touched; he has lost his inner anchor and is fainting under the hand of God. "*The spirit of a man will sustain his infirmity; but a broken spirit who can bear?*" (or "*raise up,*" Proverbs 18:14, mg.).

Nevertheless, the faithful Lord is watching the crucible. He will not permit the fiery trial to last one moment too long. Even now Job has not *renounced* God. The loyalty of his will has remained unshaken. In anguish of spirit he has reproached his Lord, but he does not *withdraw himself from His hand* and refuse to trust Him any more.

This is the holding fast of his integrity; his will remains surrendered to God to the very end. His resistance to God, if it may be called resistance, has been involuntary and mainly the outcry of nature shrinking from pain. But this does not hinder the Lord while continuing His work, as would be the case when the will *refuses* to endure any further chastening and the child of God determinedly appeals to Him to withdraw it from the crucible.

A CONTRAST

We have previously compared Job, the servant of God, with the Lord Christ, the Son of God, and noted the striking similarity of their *paths* of suffering; but at this point we need to *contrast* them and see an equally striking *dis*similarity in their *endurance* of suffering.

It has been said that "by nature we fear suffering more than sinning," and it seems to be true that

deeply inwrought in our very beings is shrinking
from pain and the false condemnation of our fellow-
men.

In contrast with Job, the whole life-pathway of the
Lord Christ shows a calm and steadfast acceptance
of all that was keenly painful to Him as man. He
humbled Himself, not only the once in taking upon
Him the form of a man but in every step of His path,
and was obedient unto death, even the death of the
cross.

Christ was led to the judgment hall, where there
gathered around Him men of the very same type as
the three friends of Job—religious men who professed to know God and were confident that they
were fit to be guides of the blind and correctors of the
foolish.

In a far greater measure than Job, the Lord Christ
had *caused the widow's heart to sing for joy,* spoken
gracious words such as man could never speak, and
spent out His life in ministry to all who were in
sorrow and trouble. Charged with blasphemy by
those who should have been His friends, and condemned as a sinner and a deceiver, Christ—unlike
Job—answered nothing, "*not so much as a word.*"
"When He suffered, He threatened not but committed
Himself to Him who judgeth righteously" (1 Peter 2:23).

Again, Christ upon the cross in His deep suffering
cries to His Father, "Thou answerest not" (Psalm
22:2–3), immediately adding, "*But Thou art holy,*" as
He rests upon the immutability of His Father's character of Love.

In contrast with the Lord, we hear Job say in his
hour of anguish, "Thou dost *not* answer me. . . . *Thou
art turned to be cruel to me,*" and he faints under the
hand of God!

CHAPTER 13

"For men to search out their own glory is not glory."
(Proverbs 25:27)

JOB'S SELF-VINDICATION

"I . . . if I . . . if my . . . if mine . . . and I. . . ." (Job 31)

AT this point it is thought that Job rose to his feet
and, lifting his hands towards heaven, took in
oriental fashion a solemn oath—the "oath of clearing."

Such an oath would not be surprising in light of
Job's present condition.

At an earlier stage of his trial, when describing his
pitiable condition to Bildad, Job had completely broken down and pleaded for pity from his friends. But
his spirit was suddenly freed and given a triumphant
faith in his living Redeemer, which afterwards anchored him in God far above all the further attacks of
his would-be helpers. He had remained with his
heart steadfastly fixed upon God *until* he began to
dwell upon his happy past! *Then* the contrast of his
present abject misery so fills his mental vision that
he loses sight of the faithfulness of God, *sinks back
into himself,* and drops into miserable self-pity and
self-absorption.

See the unhappy Job lying upon the ash-mound,
absorbed in the meditation of his sorrows. His mind
is revolving around himself, and he is sinking deeper
and deeper into despondency and despair. He has no
language to describe his misery. Weeping, he suddenly rises; he will vindicate himself, and by a solemn

declaration before Jehovah finally clear himself from all the charges brought against him by his friends.

Job's Attitude Toward Sin

"I made a covenant with mine eyes." (Job 31:1)

Job first asserts that he had made a fixed determination to so guard his eyes as not even to look at anything that might lead him into sin, and in this he shows his knowledge of one of the very first conditions for walking in fellowship with God.

The Lord Jesus plainly puts the same conditions in the laws of the Kingdom given in His Sermon on the Mount. He tells His disciples that a look and a desire is counted before God as the actual committal of the sin.

"What portion should I have of God," said Job, *"and what heritage of the El-Shaddai"* (31:2, mg.) *but calamity and disaster* (31:3) if I had been unrighteous or a worker of iniquity? *"Doth not He see my ways, and number all my steps"* (31:4)?

Job's Attitude Toward the World

"If I have walked with vanity, ... if my step hath turned out of the way, . . . then. . . ." (Job 31:5–8)

Job has kept far away from the vanity, emptiness and deceit of the world. He was sure that his heart's desire had not followed his eyes, for in spite of anything he may have been compelled to see around him, he had been separated unto God and had not touched the unclean thing (31:7). He was willing to be tried in the balances of God Himself so that his singleness of purpose in all these matters might be proved (31:6).

Job's Attitude Toward Women

"If my heart hath been enticed unto a woman, . . . then . . . ." (Job 31:9–12)

Job declares that he has always been faithful to his wife. He has already stated (31:1) that he had made "a covenant with [his] eyes" not to look lustfully at a virgin—a girl. Now he further avers that he has not allowed his "heart to be enticed" by a woman other than his wife. Nor has he ever lurked at his "neighbor's doorway" (31:9) to overhear or perhaps gaze upon some sexual activity within—such is the implication. "If I have, then may my wife grind grain for another man and become his wife—for lust is both shameful and a consuming fire, a sin to be judged," he declares (31:10–12).

Job's Attitude Toward His Neighbor

"If I did despise the cause of my manservant or of my maidservant, . . . if I have withheld aught that the poor desired, . . . if I have seen any perish for want, . . . if I have lifted up my hand against the fatherless, . . . then . . . ." (Job 31:13–22)

Job's servants had found him a good master. When they complained to him, he had always listened to their cause, remembering that he would have to give account to God as to his dealings with them (31:14); neither had he shown any pride of position, for he knew that master and servant were equal before God (31:15).

When the poor applied to Job for help, he had always responded to their need. The widow's eyes had never failed on account of him (31:16); he had not been selfish and "eaten [his] morsel alone," thinking only of his own necessities (31:17); he had not said to the needy, "Go in peace, be ye warmed and filled," and withheld from them the things needful for their bodies (31:19–20); he had never oppressed the fatherless nor taken advantage of his position of authority to crush or injure those who had no helpers (31:21). If he had transgressed against his neighbor in any of these things, he would wish that *his arm should be broken from the bone* (31:22)! He had always feared the judgments of God and lived in awe of His holiness, for His "excellency" had made him feel he must do nothing to grieve Him (31:23).

Job's Attitude Toward Wealth

"If I have made gold my hope, . . . if I rejoiced because my wealth was great, and because mine hand had gotten much. . . ." (Job 31:24–25)

Job acknowledges that God had prospered him in the things of time and had increased his substance in the land, but with sincerity of heart he could say that he had never made gold his hope or his confidence. It had not been his first object in the world, and he had never rejoiced because his wealth was great nor gloried in his possessions.

Job's Attitude Toward Idolatry

"If I beheld the sun when it shined, or the moon . . . and my heart hath been secretly enticed. . . ." (Job 31:26–27)

Job could say that he had been true to Jehovah even in the midst of the idolatry of the nations around him. He had beheld the sun and gazed upon the beauty of the moon in the starlit heavens, but his heart had never been secretly tempted to worship them. His mouth had not kissed his hand in the usual obeisance offered to the sun and moon. This would have been iniquity to him and a denial of the God that is above (31:28, mg.).

Job's Attitude Toward His Enemy

"If I rejoiced at the destruction of him that hated me. . . ." (Job 31:29)

Job could testify that he had not been "lifted up" or rejoiced in heart at the downfall of an enemy (31:29). He had been so free from the spirit of revenge that he had not permitted his mouth to sin by uttering a word that would arouse others to fight on his behalf, even though those around him had said "How nice it would be to have a piece of his flesh!" and had protested that they could not be satisfied until they made the antagonist suffer (31:31).

In brief, Job asserts that in every department of his life he had walked uprightly in integrity and singleness of heart. He had been *generous in hospitality,* opening his doors to the traveler (31:32); he had been *frank and honest* in confession of transgression, never covering over iniquity after the manner of men (31:33, mg.); he had been *fearless* of the multitude, never swerving from the path of right through terror of contempt and ignominy, or hiding himself in his own tent and fearing to open his mouth (31:34). He had lived his life straight before God and men.

About eighty times do the personal pronouns *I, my, me, mine,* occur in Job's long self-vindication, and he concludes it with the words, *"Lo, here is my signature, let the Almighty answer me"* (31:35).

Job was prepared to sign his name to every word that he had said; even more, if he had the indictment before him that his prosecutor had written against him (31:35), he would lift it upon his shoulder, accept it as a *crown* (31:36) and in princely dignity "present it to him" (31:37, mg.), declaring even to his face that his steps had been in the way of the Lord.

Yet one word more Job wishes to say: If there are any crying out against me, if I have grasped for myself or caused others to suffer on account of *me* (31:38–39), then "let thorns grow instead of wheat, and noisome weeds instead of barley" (31:40, mg.).

"The words of Job are ended."

The Silenced Friends!

"So these three men ceased to answer Job, because he was righteous in his own eyes." (Job 32:1)

The Spirit of God did not bear witness to Job's self-vindication. The friends were silenced but not convinced! The attempt to clear his own character *appeared to them as self-righteousness,* so that he brought dishonor upon himself and failed to glorify God.

Job had undoubtedly walked with a conscience void of offense toward God and man, but the persistent accusations of his friends, added to his keen physical, mental, as well as spiritual sufferings, had stung him into a *self-defense* that was contrary to the spirit of true effacement.

No child of God can safely vindicate his own integrity. God alone can bear witness as the soul humbly leaves his character in His hands. But the very language of Job's self-vindication shows that he needed the refining fire. It unveils an aspect of the subtle life of self that only reveals itself *after* an experience of power and fruitful service, for *each stage of spiritual growth has its own temptations and perils.*

In the furnace of trial the soul is put to the most

extreme test the All-seeing Lord knows it can endure so that the hidden depths of one's character may be revealed. Job had borne a prolonged and most searching trial. He had shown in the furnace a submission to the will of God and a tenacious faith in Him which were both beautiful; a clearness of conscience and an endurance of suffering which were wonderful. But Job also showed that he was unknowingly allowing the gifts of God to become *more to him than the will of God*, and was in danger of grasping to himself the very power that God had given him, thus making it appear to others that he was righteous in his own eyes.

The Apostle Paul walked with God as closely as Job had done, and yet how different his language about himself. And remember that he lived in the furnace of trial from the *first hour* of his knowledge of God.

"*I know nothing against myself*," writes Paul to the Corinthians, "yet am I *not* hereby justified: but He that judgeth me is the *Lord*" (1 Corinthians 4:4).

CHAPTER 14

"Then said I, Ah, Lord God! behold, I cannot speak:
for I am a child. But the Lord said, . . . On whatsoever
errand I shall send thee thou shalt go." (Jeremiah 1:6–
7, mg.)

ELIHU
THE MESSENGER OF GOD

"Then was kindled the wrath of Elihu . . . against
Job, . . . because he justified himself rather than God."
(Job 33:2)

LISTENING to all that had passed between Job and
his friends was a younger man named Elihu. He
has not been mentioned before, possibly because he
was considered too young to be noticed; nevertheless,
from Elihu's speech it is apparent that he possessed a
spiritual discernment unknown by the older men.

How slow we are to heed the repeated declarations
of the Scriptures that God hides His secrets from the
wise of this world and reveals them unto babes. He
chooses the weak and despised so that no flesh may
glory before Him.

Joseph is taught of God and led through suffering
to the throne, while his elder brethren are left to be
shepherds in Goshen.

The "*little ones*" cross the Jordan into the promised
land, while the unbelieving elders die in the wilderness.

David is chosen to be the anointed king of Israel
over the heads of his elder brethren, comely as they

were; and in this ancient story we see the young
Elihu chosen as God's messenger to the afflicted Job.

Elihu's Modesty

> "Elihu . . . said, I am young, and ye are very old;
> wherefore I held back, and durst not show you mine
> opinion. I said, Days should speak." (Job 32:6-7)

It is pleasant to notice Elihu's modesty and tact in
entering into the painful discussion he had listened
to between his elders.

It is written that his "wrath was kindled" against
Job and the three friends (32:5). This is explained by
his words later on about the constraining of the
Spirit within him so that he was, as he says, "ready
to burst."

Ezekiel refers to this "heat of the spirit" when the
hand of the Lord was strong upon him.

Such heat of the spirit may well have been kindled
in Elihu against Job and his friends, for he perceived
as he listened that Job was becoming more and more
concerned about clearing his own character rather
than justifying the love and wisdom of God in laying
His hand upon him.

Elihu saw, too, that the aged friends had utterly
failed to find an answer to Job's complaints or to
explain to him God's purpose in placing him in the
crucible, and yet they had condemned him without
mercy (32:3).

Elihu is conscious that he is in a very delicate
position for a young man. How is he to speak to these
dignified seniors? He holds himself back and watches
for the right moment (32:4). If the Spirit of God has
chosen him to be the interpreter, he will wait until He
opens the way for him. At last there is a pause. The
friends "cease to answer Job" and "the words of Job
are ended."

The constraining hand of God comes upon Elihu, and he opens his lips. He takes at once the lowly place, acknowledges his youthfulness, and confesses how he had shrunk from saying what was in his mind before such great men. But he knows that there is "a spirit in man," and it is "the breath of the Almighty" alone that gives understanding (32:8) and not position or age (32:9); therefore he would venture to say, *"Hearken to me"* though he was but a young man (32:10).

Having thus cleared the ground, Elihu speaks out boldly. He had waited and listened attentively to every word that the older men had "searched out what to say" in reasoning with Job (32:11), but he had seen that they had utterly failed to convince him. Wise and aged men as they were, he could only account for this by thinking that God meant to vanquish Job Himself, lest the friends should glory in their own wisdom (32:12–13, mg.). Job had said no word directly to him; therefore he would not attempt to answer all that he had said as the friends had done (32:14).

Having spoken thus far, Elihu pauses and looks for some word of encouragement from his audience, but no response comes from the astonished elders. *"They are amazed; . . . they have not a word to say,"* he exclaims (32:15). *"Shall I wait, because they speak not?"* (32:16) he cries. No, the frigid silence must not make him unfaithful to God; he must fulfill his part in God's purposes and not withhold the light that has been given him (32:17).

The older men had been obliged to search out "what to say," and when they had found something with much labor, it was powerless and unconvincing; but Elihu, the messenger of God, was "full of words." The Spirit within was constraining him and pouring the message into his mind so that he would have to

speak to find relief (32:18–20, mg.). However much
he shrank back and felt the position he was placed
in, he had no alternative but to deliver the burden
upon his soul. He would beg their forbearance if he
did not speak as respectfully as he would wish to do,
but he desired not to so "respect any man's person"
as to prevent him giving the message of God (32:21).
He did not know how to give "flattering titles," and if
he allowed the dignity of his audience to hinder his
faithfulness, his Maker would soon put him aside
(32:22).

Elihu as God's Messenger

> "Howbeit, Job, I pray thee, hear my speech; . . . my
> words shall utter the uprightness of my heart: and
> that which my lips know they shall speak sincerely."
> (Job 33:1–3)

With courtesy Elihu now addresses himself to Job
and beseeches him to hearken to his message. He
has opened his mouth in obedience to the constraining of the Spirit, and he would speak frankly, honestly, and sincerely that which he knew and no more.
He dared to speak to Job because he knew that the
Spirit of God had made him and the *breath of the
Almighty* had given him life (33:4). Should Job desire
to refute him, he urges him to set forth his case yet
again (33:5). As far as he himself was concerned, he,
like Job, was *"formed out of the clay"* (33:6); therefore
he would not be hard upon him, and Job need not be
afraid of him (33:7). But Job had expressed a wish
for an umpire, one who would stand between God
and himself; therefore, *according to his wish*, Elihu
would be to Job *"in God's stead"* (33:6, mg.) and
reason the case with him; he would seek to be a
mouthpiece for God.

Elihu's Summary of Job's Position

> "Thou hast spoken in mine hearing . . . saying, I am
> clean. . . . I am innocent. . . . He findeth occasions
> against me. He counteth me for His enemy. . . . Behold,
> . . . in this thou art not just." (Job 33:8–12)

Elihu rapidly sums up the case and uses Job's
very words for the purpose, saying that according to
these *he* was innocent and God was dealing with him
as an *enemy*! Job had said that in the old days his
"justice" had been as a diadem upon his head, but in
this matter his sense of right had forsaken him.
Ought he, a finite man, thus to judge one so infinite
as Jehovah? Did he expect God to give an account of
His matters to him, however sadly he misjudged Him
(33:13)? How foolish to *strive against Him,* for no
struggling and writhing would compel Him to speak.

Elihu is manifestly under the Spirit's guidance in
this wise dealing with Job. Rapidly and clearly does
the Spirit of God reveal to His messengers the condition of the souls He sends them to. Elihu's quick
grasp of the heart of the matter is in striking contrast
to the vain reasonings of the older men, searching
out what to say, pouring out torrents of words far
away from the real need, utterly, hopelessly blind to
the true diagnosis of the case. *Touchy* were they
when their wisdom was doubted, *self-assertive* of
knowledge, *hard* in application of a theory—overrid-
ing even all the principles of humanity in their determination to prove their case.

Elihu passes by all the side issues, ignores all the
theoretical discussion, and says in effect: Then it
comes to this, Job, *you* are innocent, and all the
wrong is on *God's side*!

If there is blame at all, you place it upon *Him*!
Where is your sense of right? Just think a moment.
You are placing the Lord of Hosts in an impossible

position. As your Creator He cannot yield to your demand. Why enter into a battle with Him? He cannot give an account to you of His dealings. Why put Him into the place of an enemy by taking the attitude of an enemy yourself!

How God Speaks

> "God speaketh in one way, yea, in two, though man regardeth [perceiveth, A.V.] it not." (Job 33:14, mg.)

Elihu had said that no agonizing or striving on Job's part would compel Jehovah to give an account of His actions, but this did not mean that God never spoke at all. The trouble was that men did not *understand* His way of speaking nor give sufficient heed to regarding His voice. They were "dull of hearing" and did not *perceive* His workings.

Elihu would explain to Job two different methods which the Lord employed in instructing His children—two "classes," so to speak, in His school for training them to know Him and His will. One was by the direct inner teaching of the Holy Spirit in the heart. "*In a dream, in a vision of the night,*" when the child of God in deep slumber upon the bed (33:15) is separated from earthly duties and interests, the blessed Spirit gently uncovers the inner ear of the heart and seals the instruction of Jehovah upon it as a seal stamps its impression upon melted wax (33:16).

The Lord explains to Job by the mouth of Elihu the characteristics of the true teaching of the Spirit of God in contrast to the vision described to him by Eliphaz.

The contrast is very striking. How gentle is the work of the Holy Spirit as He softly opens the inward ear and presses upon the receptive heart the "*instruction of the Lord*"—even as it was promised in after days, "I will put My law in their inward parts, and in their heart will I write it" (Jeremiah 31:33).

How frightening was the "vision" described by Eliphaz. Fear, trembling, and shaking came upon him, and the hair of his flesh stood up with horror as a "form" passed before his eyes, and he heard a voice whispering to him a subtle doubt about the character of God.

The Lord Jesus was the perfect pattern of the servant with the opened ear, for He said of His Father, "*He wakeneth Me morning by morning, He wakeneth Mine ear to hear as they that are taught*" (Isaiah 50:4).

This gentle instruction sealed upon the heart by the Eternal Spirit has been called by old writers the "*diffused knowledge of God*" and marks the stage of what has been described as the "Unitive way" of fellowship with Him, in contrast to an earlier stage called the "Illuminative way," when light is given rather to the mind.

The silent instruction of the Holy Spirit described by Elihu is only possible to a heart truly and wholly surrendered to God and made soft and plastic as wax melted before the fire. All struggling under the hand of God must have ceased and the will have been brought into quiet harmony with His, with a clear atmosphere between the soul and Him all through the duties of the day.

The Object of All God's Speaking

"That He may withdraw man *from his purpose,* and hide pride from man; that He *keep back his soul from the pit,* and his life from perishing by the sword." (Job 33:17–18, mg.)

Self-will and pride describe the two strongest characteristics of fallen man as inherited from the first Adam.

The second Adam, the Lord from heaven, completed the work of redemption upon Calvary's cross, but what long patience is needed with every soul before the fruit of that blessed work is seen and the redeemed are truly conformed to the image of the Son.

How long is the patient waiting of the Lord before the citadel of the will is gained for the Redeemer; but how much longer does He watch and work before the whole being is so possessed by Him that His blood-bought ones are content to fulfill simply and only the will of God.

The desires of the heart may have been cleansed by the power of the precious blood of Jesus so that the *choice* of the soul may be the grace of true humility, yet the continuing work of God is needed to remove pride from man and enable him to renounce himself and his own life so as to share in the life abundant of his Lord and thus be kept from a lost or wasted life.

The School of Suffering

"He is chastened also with pain. . . . His soul draweth near unto the pit, and his life to the destroyers." (Job 33:19, 22)

Elihu now describes another way in which God speaks to His children when the soul, first taught of God in the heart, is placed in the school of suffering* and "chastened also with pain."

The words of Elihu confirm Job's belief that his sufferings have come from the hand of God, for Elihu says it is the *Lord* who speaks to the one chastened with pain that He may keep back his soul from the pit.

The word "chastened" here is literally *convicted,*

---

* With God, speaking is *doing* and He only explains His designs by putting the soul in the crucible—*Guyon.*

although in almost every other passage of Scripture it means "to instruct" or "train up" as a parent trains a child.*

The soul in the school of suffering is *convicted* by strong pain. How deep the conviction is when the lessons of the All-wise Father are burned in as it were by fire!

That "man may *put away his purpose*" (33:17, mg.)—or his plans!—the Lord withdraws him from his work, lays His hand upon him, strips him of all his natural vigor and strength so that he loses desire for bread or even "dainty meat" (33:20). His outward man wastes away until nought but the "bodily frame" of the earthly tent is seen (33:21). His soul is poured out until he lies at the very edge of the grave; his life hangs as it were by a thread; and the destroyers—angels of death commissioned to end man's life (Fausset)—wait for permission to exercise their power, for the Lord Christ holds the keys of death, and none can pass through the gates of death without His word.

The servant of God is face to face with eternity. The "work" he has been withdrawn from disappears into the dim and fading past. The surrender to God in days of strength is tested. Does he truly desire the *will* of God above the *work* of God? Is he willing to be henceforth a *broken* vessel so that the excellency of the power may be seen to be of God? Will he glory in his *weakness* that the power of Christ may rest upon him?

Happy are the souls who are ready to reply, "Most gladly, Lord!" "*Most gladly, therefore,* will I rather *glory in my weaknesses* that the strength of Christ may cover me" (2 Corinthians 12:9, mg.).

Happy are the souls who thus have looked within

---

* See 1 Corinthians 11:32, 2 Corinthians 6:9, Hebrews 12:5–11, Revelation 3:19.

the gates and found God all in all!

It must not be assumed that the picture drawn by Elihu of the teaching of God in the school of suffering needs be fulfilled *in detail* in the experience of every soul. The picture is a general one, expressing the simple lesson that the All-wise Father teaches His children by afflictions as well as by the direct heart-instruction of His Spirit, dealing with each one according to his character and need, so that out of the furnace there may come forth *"a vessel for the finer."*

Without doubt there are depths in every soul only to be reached in the school of suffering, and they who shrink back from following their Lord in learning obedience by *the things which they suffer* will remain unmellowed and untaught in the richest and deepest knowledge of God.

We must not forget also that the picture drawn by Elihu may be fulfilled in a *spiritual* sense even in the midst of the "work" entrusted to the servant of God. There may be an inward and spiritual stripping of strength and power, a loss of keen desire for the spiritual bread, a pouring out of the soul even unto death, a detaching from the "work" and the things of earth while in their very midst—known but to God alone.

Be it in any way that God wills, the lessons of the crucible must be learned.

The servant of God must be taught to rejoice in the *will of God* rather than his service for God, and to glory in *weakness* as a condition for knowing the divine strength brought to its full development of power.

The faithful servant of God must even be willing to suffer many things for the sake of being *fitted for empathetic ministry to other souls,* even as it is written that Christ Himself in glory, as our High Priest, is *touched* with the *feeling of our weaknesses* because on earth He was in all points tried even as those He came to save.

CHAPTER 15

"Think it not strange concerning the fiery trial . . . which cometh upon you to prove you, as though a strange thing happened unto you." (1 Peter 4:12)

THE MESSAGE
OF THE RANSOM

"Deliver him; . . . I have found a Ransom." (Job 33:24)

ELIHU has described the condition of the soul in the school of pain brought down to the very gates of death.

Sometimes the gates are opened, and the suffering one passes through to higher service not having even *seen* death, for death is swallowed up in victory even as mortality is swallowed up in life.

Some gaze within the gates and are sent back to fulfill their ministry on earth in the light of the face of Him who conquered death.

Elihu says, *"If there be with him . . . an interpreter"* (33:23). The thought in the original is very suggestive. The word means *"to treat as a foreigner."* The child of God does not understand the language in which his Father is speaking to him! He has known the instruction of the Spirit in the heart, but now he needs an "interpreter," one taught of God to explain the lessons of the crucible.

The word "interpreter" is interchangeable with *ambassador* in Isaiah 43 (v. 27, mg.). The interpreter is also an ambassador from the King of kings, one who

147

knows how to commune with the King and is chosen by Him to convey His message and speak with authority in His name.

Elilhu says that such interpreters are "*one among a thousand.*" They are rare because few are willing for the necessary training in the school of suffering and the furnace seven times heated, which develops in the soul that sensitive intuition of the mind of God and delicate touch with the Spirit of God needed for such a work.

The friends of Job could *search out words* from their store of knowledge, and in beautiful language *reason, so they thought,* on God's behalf. But they could not understand Job's position nor interpret to him the purposes of God in placing him in the crucible.

"An interpreter . . . *to show unto man what is right for him.*" Elihu has plainly shown Job what was right for him to do: the searching of his own heart and the self-consolation that he had not knowingly transgressed against the Lord *must end.* The misjudging of God in thinking that He was treating His servant as an enemy *must be put away.* The writhing under His hand must *cease.* For until he ended the struggling and rested upon the faithfulness of God, there was no hope of response or light from Him upon his path.

The Word of the Cross

> "Then He is gracious unto him, and saith, Deliver him; . . . *I have found a Ransom.*" (Job 33:24)

It has often been said that the Old Testament contains the germ of the New. The Ransom spoken of by Elihu is unmistakably the Ransom proclaimed by the Apostle Paul, who saw with marvelous spiritual vision that the sacrifice of Christ *began in far-back ages of eternity,* declaring that He gave Himself a Ransom for all, the "testimony" to be "borne in its own times."

Elilhu may not have known the full prophetical import of his message, for we are told by the Apostle Peter that the prophets searched diligently what time "*the Spirit of Christ which was in them* did point unto when it *testified beforehand* the sufferings of Christ" (1 Peter 1:11).

Peter's words show that the *Spirit of Christ was in Elihu* as he preached deliverance through the Ransom to the afflicted Job. Thus we have, in the oldest book extant, the germ of the after-revealed gospel and the foreshadowed message of the cross.

Elihu was a true messenger of God to Job. Without superfluity of words he interprets to him his position and gives the message of life.

God has been leading Job to another class in His school: from the stage of the instruction of the heart to the lessons of the crucible. He had withdrawn him from the work he loved that He might save him from spiritual pride, so that nothing in his life might end in corruption or perish under the judgments of God.

God had brought him down from his high place to make him know himself and his dependence upon Him for every breath of life. Now, at the point of extremity, let him take the right attitude before the Lord, cease from himself, and think no more of his own integrity but turn away to his Redeemer.

Job had seen his Redeemer as the Living One who would vindicate him in the day of His coming, but let him now see Him as *the Ransom,* the One who would be gracious to him and deliver him from going down to the pit—*not on the ground of Job's integrity* but on the ground of His own sacrifice for the redemption of fallen man.

"*I have found a Ransom*" is now the message of God to Job, *foreshadowing the "word of the cross"* preached by the Apostle Paul: "to them that are perishing, foolishness; but unto us which are being saved . . . the power of God."

Job had been placed by the will of God in a crucible of unparalleled trial. In the anguish of his sufferings there was revealed an aspect of the life of self not seen in his days of prosperity and power. The turning point of his deliverance must therefore come to him by a fresh appropriation of the "Ransom"—the death of the Son of God.

Through this atoning sacrifice alone can *grace, mercy, and peace* flow to the stripped and suffering soul and the omnipotent word be spoken: "Deliver him; . . . *I have found a Ransom.*"

The Life Out of Death

"His flesh shall be fresher than a child's; he returneth to the days of his youth." (Job 33:25)

The omnipotent word of deliverance through the Ransom is followed by the impartation of the new life in Christ Jesus, sweet and fresh as a little child's.

In another part of the Old Testament, and again in a living object lesson, we have a corresponding passage to this message of Elihu to Job.

Naaman was bidden to wash seven times in the waters of Jordan, and then his flesh "came again like unto the flesh of a little child" (2 Kings 5:14).

The Ransom preached to Job and the waters of Jordan commanded to Naaman both *prefigure the death on Calvary's cross,* and in each case the result of believing obedience is seen to be the same.

The *objective* work of Christ is proclaimed to Job for his deliverance, even as we understand that by faith we are truly one with Christ upon His cross and in the sight of God have died in Him.

The *subjective* aspect of the death of Christ is more

clearly seen in Naaman's story, for he was bidden go into Jordan seven times before he could emerge in the likeness of a little child. The "seven times" express simply the lesson that we need the many times into Jordan before we lose the pride of life in knowledge and power and become one of the little ones who are the greatest in the Kingdom of heaven.

Surely Job's prolonged path of trial must have meant to him a very real passing through the waters of Jordan.

He had been such a great man; how could he ever become as a little child while he retained his place as chief and sat as a king among his troops?

The Child-Access to God

"He prayeth unto God, and He is favourable unto him; so that he seeth His face with joy: and He restoreth unto man his righteousness." (Job 33:26)

Job had known in his days of fellowship with God what it was to call upon Him and receive the answer, but through the fiery trial that he has called "strange" he is being led into a life of child-communion with the Father such as he has not known before.

Job had looked back upon the past and remembered how the friendship of God had been with him in his tent, but in the richer and fuller life that God is calling him to he is to have *access to Him in His sanctuary*, behold his face with joy, and know that he has whatsoever petition he desires of Him.

God will restore unto him once more the assurance of righteousness before Him, "*accepted in the Beloved*," the Ransom who purchased him with His own blood.

The Child-Honesty Before Men

"He looketh upon men, and saith, *I have sinned*, . . . and it was not requited unto me. He hath redeemed

my soul from going into the pit, and my life shall behold the light." (Job 33:27–28, mg.)

Job, in the consciousness of his heart integrity
before God, resented being charged with transgression by his friends. "*Tell me* where I have erred," he
cries; and "*if* I have sinned, . . . why dost Thou not
pardon me?" he pleads with God.

Unable to confess to any of the definite charges
brought against him by Eliphaz, he can only say "*I
have not gone back,*" and finally close the discussion
with the words, "*My heart doth not reproach me for
any of my days.*" "*Till I die I will not put away mine
integrity from me; my righteousness I hold fast, and
will not let it go.*"

At the beginning of the story of Job's fiery trial, we
have seen him to be intensely sensitive to every
possibililty of grieving the Lord. With his whole heart
he "shunned evil" and offered sacrifices to God for
even the sins of ignorance of his children. Hence his
inability to understand the dealings of God with him
and why *he* should have been placed—the just and
wholehearted man—in such a furnace of trial. Gleams
of light at times have broken upon him, and the
thought of gold being placed in the fire for the refining away of the dross comes to his mind; but his last
words to the friends show that, regardless, he is sure
of his integrity before God and is determined to cling
to that assurance to the end.

The Spirit-taught interpreter, Elihu, shows that he
has understood the dealings of God with Job, but he
does not attempt to combat his insistence on integrity as the other men have done. He only tells him
that the soul who has learned to know himself in the
school of trial and has turned in utter self-despair to
the Ransom in his hour of need will come out, not
only with a *new spirit as a little child,* a *new fresh-*

ness of life in heavenly youthfulness, a *new power in prayer* and *joyous knowledge of the face of God,* a *new assurance of righteousness in union with the Righteous One,* but also with a *new attitude toward sin* and *honest confession of sin to others.*

With unspeakable relief the childlike spirit can leave the character of its Father to His own keeping and know that it need no longer strain to uphold its testimony to His delivering power. It need not fear *to frankly own up when it is wrong* and to say plainly to men, *"I have sinned,* and it was not requited unto me" (33:27, mg.).

The delivered one *"singeth before men"* as he looks back upon the gracious dealings of God with him, for he sees how he has been redeemed from the pit of nothingness, and with glad new hopes he cries, *"My life shall behold the light"* (33:28)!

The Thrice Working of God

"Lo, all these things doth God *work,* twice, *yea, thrice,* with a man, to bring back his soul from the pit, that he may be enlightened with the light of life." (Job 33:29–30, mg.)

Elihu had said that God "speaketh in one way, yea, in two" (33:14) and had described His two classes for the instruction of His children, but he now says that He *works all these things twice* and *thrice* with a man, bringing his soul from the pit and enlightening him with the light of the living.

Is this one of the gleams of light that so wondrously bring out the inner harmony of the sacred writings?

The "three days" so often met with in various parts of Scripture is generally understood to typify the death and resurrection of Christ. The Lord Himself said, "As Jonah was three days and three nights in the . . . sea-monster, so shall the Son of Man be three days and three nights in the heart of the earth" (Matthew 12:40, mg.). So does Elihu's language mean that God works the "twice" in bringing souls into fellowship with Christ in His death, but that the "thrice" of "resurrection" is needed before they know the abundant life in union with the Risen Lord?

In any case, the *purpose* of the patient working of God is emphasized as the *delivering of the soul from the pit* (see Isaiah 38:17, mg.) and the life from perishing by the sword.

Elihu speaks again and again of the *soul* and the *life* and always connects the *soul* with the *"pit."*

It is important to distinguish things that differ. When the Scripture speaks of the soul, it does not mean the *spirit.*

Paul describes the threefold nature of man as spirit, soul and body, and explains the difference between soul and spirit in his letter to the Corinthians when he says that "the first Adam became a living soul. The last Adam became a life-giving Spirit" (1 Corinthians 15:45–46).

Again the word of God in its workings is said to *divide between soul and spirit,* piercing as a sharp knife to the very joints and marrow of the inner being of man (Hebrews 4:12).

In speaking of the grain of wheat falling into the ground to die, Christ said, "He that loveth his life [soul] loseth it; and he that hateth his life [soul] in this world shall keep it unto life eternal" (John 12:25, mg.).

The soul-life therefore is the life that we derive from the first Adam, the fallen life of nature. The second Adam, the Lord from heaven, quickens the *spirit* and brings it into union with Himself as a life-giving Spirit. Dwelling within, in the shrine of the spirit, the Master Workman then divides *between soul and spirit* by the Word of God, which reveals the soul-life in its true light so that it may be unswervingly "hated" or renounced and surrendered to the death of the cross, where it is continually exchanged for life eternal in union with the Risen Lord.

These New Testament passages throw strong light upon Elihu's message to Job at this particular point of his spiritual history.

Job's integrity of heart is beyond question. He has known fellowship with God, and the Spirit of God has dwelt within him and given him life. In the crucible, *soul and spirit are being divided* until the soul-life *mingled with his service for God* is brought to light, being revealed in the self-vindicating that broke from him at the crucial point of his trial.

After the wondrous Spirit-given interpretation of God's way of teaching His children, Elihu appeals to Job to mark well the message (33:31) and earnestly entreats him to speak, for he truly desires to "justify" him or help him to understand God's way with him (33:32).

But Job is silent.

CHAPTER 16

"Is the Spirit of the Lord impatient? Are these His doings?" (Micah 2:7, mg.)

ELIHU THE MAN

"Moreover Elihu answered and said, Hear my words, ye wise men." (Job 34:1–2)

ELIHU waits for some response from Job, but in vain; he remains silent.

Turning then to the friends, Elihu appeals to them as men with knowledge (34:2), wise men, to listen to what he had to say, for *"the ear trieth words, as the palate tasteth meat"* (34:3).

Leaving Job severely alone, Elihu begs the older men to search out this matter with him. For if Job will not acknowledge what is right, "Let *us* choose. . . . Let *us* know among ourselves what is good" (34:4), he says, as he proceeds to discuss Job's attitude and Job's language before his face!

Elihu himself is in evidence at this point of the story. In interpreting the ways of God and proclaiming deliverance through the Ransom to the afflicted Job, he is manifestly under the power of the Eternal Spirit, speaking with modest diffidence and tactful tenderness; but when he has poured out his heart and no response comes, his self-sensitiveness appears to be touched; he thinks Job's silence to be scorn, and cries, *"What man is like Job, who drinketh up scorning like water?"* (34:7).

The messenger of God needs *the patience of God* as

well as the message! Elihu was so sure that he had the light of the Spirit upon Job's path that he probably expected an immediate result from all that he had said, but why did he not quietly give the word and go his way? Why did he fail to understand the fitness of things and remember Job's position with the aged listeners looking on? Why did Elihu *expect* Job to confess that the word had met his need? *God had humbled him*; it was not for Elihu to add one jot to the humiliation!

Elihu was deeply taught in the ways of God, but this failure in patience suggests the question whether he himself had personally been through the school of suffering he had depicted so vividly to Job; for after a measure of growth the soul becomes able to discern spiritual things quickly, and then it is easy for *the light to outrun the experience,* the lack of the corresponding life-power betraying itself in some critical moment just as it appears to have done in Elihu when he is tested by the silence of Job.

In dealing with others, how often we fail as Elihu did! If the soul yields at once to our message, we are full of joy; but if through some reserve of temperament or intensity of feeling it is speechless, we lose patience, attribute the dumbness to some wrong cause, lose touch with the gentle working of the Holy Spirit, and finally leave the soul unhelped or cast down into deeper despair.

Elihu delivers his message; and then, when Job is silent, pours forth a multitude of words from his own mind to emphasize the message he had been given, instead of quietly leaving the word with God, who would "watch over [His] word to perform it." Again, we do the same in the work of God today! We cooperate with the Lord up to a point, carefully and slowly depending upon Him for every word, and upon the Holy Spirit to bear witness and hold the attention of the listeners. But often we fail to discern *when the message has been delivered* and add a multitude of words from our own minds to explain or press home the message from God.

Elihu's Torrent of Words

> "Job hath said, I am righteous. . . . What man is like Job? . . . He hath said, It profiteth a man nothing that he should delight himself with God." (Job 34:5–9)

The difference between Elihu the *interpreter* and Elihu the *man* is very plainly to be seen. Elihu appears to have been wounded by the persistent silence of Job and his friends. In his self-hurt he ceases to speak on God's behalf, loses his quiet restraint, and begins to make charges against Job as the elder men had done.

Elihu complains that Job persists in thinking his wound to be incurable (34:6). It was evident that Job scorned all efforts to help him! If he had not transgressed himself, he must have *associated* with workers of iniquity and walked with wicked men (34:8)! "*For he hath said,*" quoted Elihu, "*It profiteth a man nothing that he should delight himself with God*" (34:9).

Job had said nothing of the kind as regards himself. The words Elihu quoted were words that Job had used descriptive of the attitude of the ungodly toward the Almighty (21:15)!

Elihu's relapse into sensitive self-consciousness has brought a dimness of spiritual vision and power. His tactfulness has gone, his poise of spirit, his gentle courtesy, and even his sense of exact truth and justice in quoting Job's words.

Elihu proceeds to "*teach wisdom*" to the aged friends, and he takes up very much the same line of argument as they had done at the beginning.

God is so great, so holy that He will not do wickedness (34:10); according to the *work* of a man *would He render unto Him* (34:11); His judgment would be absolutely right (34:12); He was the sovereign Lord of the whole world (34:13); He could *withdraw the breath* from all men and cause them to turn again to the dust (34:14–15). Should men dare to condemn One so just and mighty (34:17)? Was it seemly to say even to an earthly king, "Thou art vile"?—how much less to Him who respected not persons nor regarded the rich more than the poor (34:18–19)? All are the work of His hands and die in a moment even though they appear to be mighty (34:20). His eyes see all the ways of men, and none can hide themselves from Him (34:21–22). *He breaketh the mighty in ways past finding out,* puts others in their stead and overturns their works (34:24–25). He strikes them in the open sight of others because they have turned aside from following Him and caused the cry of the poor to come unto Him (34:26–28). *When He gave quietness, there were none who could condemn* (or *make trouble*), and when He pleased to hide His face there were none who could behold (34:29, A.V.). He deals the same with a nation as with a man, for He is the Lord of the whole earth and will not allow a godless man to rule lest the people be ensnared (34:29–30).

Surely, Elihu continues, the only right attitude before such a God is a humble accepting of His chastening, saying, *"I will not offend any more. That which I see not, teach Thou me. If I have done iniquity, I will do it no more"* (34:31–32). Did Job expect a recompense to suit himself if he refused to take this attitude? It was Job himself who had to choose and not Elihu. If Job *would* but speak (34:33)! But every wise man listening would agree that Job had spoken before without knowledge and without wisdom (34:34–35)!

Job continues dumb, and Elihu loses patience still more. Since Job treated with silent scorn all efforts to help him, he could only say, *"My father, let Job be tried unto the end, . . . for he addeth rebellion unto his sin"* (34:36–37, mg.).

Elihu's Severity

"Thou sayest, . . . What profit shall I have?" (Job 35:3)

Elihu continues addressing the silent Job and tries to refute the expression he *thinks* he has used about the profit of serving God. He is attempting, it seems, to read Job's mind and deduce his motives. Job had never thought about "advantage" or "profit" in his service to Jehovah, but he will not open his lips to set Elihu right, and allows him to go on with his torrent of words against the man of straw he has set up. Elihu's language to the afflicted man takes a severe tone, and he ceases to speak with the deference and respect becoming his youth.

"Sayest thou, My righteousness is more than God's?" (35:2), said Elihu; *"I will answer thee, and thy companions"* (35:4). See the heavens and "behold the skies, which are higher than thou; if thou hast sinned, *what doest thou against Him"* who dwells therein (35:5–6)? The great God is above being injured or profited by men's doings (35:7). Men may be hurt by another's wickedness or profited by another's right actions, but not so the infinite God above (35:8).

Elihu sadly thinks of the selfishness of men in regard to the things of God. When they are in trouble and oppression, they cry out for help (35:9), but they do not seek after God or desire to know Him because He is their Maker and gives songs of deliverance in the night of their sorrows (35:10). Yet He had made man and desired to teach him and make him wiser than the fowls of heaven (35:11)!

It was true also that men may cry out, but God will not

answer because of their pride and vain talk (35:12–13, mg.).

Job's case was still pending before the Lord (35:14); let him wait God's pleasure. God had not yet visited Job in anger nor taken full notice of his arrogance (35:15).

Elihu concludes, once again, that Job was guilty of opening his mouth without knowing what he was saying (35:16).

CHAPTER 17

"If thou take forth the precious from the vile, thou shalt be as My mouth." (Jeremiah 15:19)

ELIHU THE INTERPRETER ONCE MORE

"Elihu . . . said, Suffer me a little, . . . I have yet somewhat to say on God's behalf." (Job 36:1–2)

THERE is a marked change in Elihu's language at this point. He resumes his courteous deference of speech and gently says, *"Suffer me a little, I have yet somewhat to say on God's behalf."*

Has he discovered that he had been speaking on his *own* behalf ever since he ceased to interpret the working of God to Job and began personally to attack him in this way? It was not seemly for him to address his elders and deal directly with all that he saw wrong *nor was it his place to apply* the message of God.

The Lord could use him to give light upon Job's path as long as he retained his modest demeanor and did not transgress the bounds of courtesy and love; but when the subtle self-sensitiveness had crept in, as a "fly in the ointment," he had been hurt with the silent reception of the message and had lost touch with the blessed Spirit of God.

Moreover, while Elihu spoke from the standpoint of an instrument—a mouthpiece for God, *"in God's stead"*—all his words were directed by the Spirit; but when his attitude was changed and he spoke as one *retained to plead for God,* he lost the marked power of God upon him.

This difference in standpoint is an important one for all who seek to be faithful servants of Jehovah. In speaking *for God,* the special pleader assumes the listener to be in the position of an antagonist to be won over to the Lord's side; but by the servant who is *only a mouthpiece,* with the lips yielded to Him for *His use,* the hearer is brought into direct dealing with God *Himself,* having contact with Him through the instrument.

Elihu resumes his right attitude toward the suffering Job, and having returned to the position of an interpreter, "*speaking in God's stead,*" the change in his tone and language is very striking. The hand of God is upon him again as he proceeds to "*ascribe righteousness to* [*his*] *Maker*" (36:3).

Much that Elihu now says is an elaboration of his first message about the two classes of instruction in the Lord's school for training His children. He will again fetch his knowledge "*from afar*"; furthermore, the One who is "*perfect in knowledge*" is with Job to enable him to recognize that the words of Elihu are true and right (36:4).

The Heart of God

> "Behold God is mighty, and despiseth not any: He is mighty in strength of heart." (Job 36:5, mg.)

Elihu is truly speaking from the right standpoint now as he tells Job that although the Lord is mighty, yet He *despises not* any of the weakest of His children. He knows their frame and remembers that they are dust. In all their affliction *He* is afflicted, yet His strength of heart-love toward them enables Him to bear seeing them suffer for their eternal gain, giving "to the afflicted their right" (36:6) after His purpose of love is accomplished.

"*He withdraweth not His eyes*" from His loved ones, but "*with kings upon the throne He setteth them for ever*" (36:7).

Elihu's message is wondrously in accord with the New Testament Scriptures, which unveil the marvelous purpose of God for His redeemed, who are chosen to be kings and priests unto Him in Christ Jesus their Lord. This is the "*right*" of the afflicted, for it is written, "*If so be* [*they*] *suffer with Him,*" they shall be also "*glorified together.*" Even thus does the Lord lift the beggar from the dunghill to set him among princes. In His purpose of love He has already set the "righteous," who are in union with the righteous One, upon the throne of victory with their Lord; and He is "*mighty in strength of heart*" in patiently fitting them for their future position; therefore He places them in the furnace that they may be prepared for their high and heavenly calling, and learn to overcome even as their Lord has overcome and sat down with His Father in His throne.

The Kingly Soul in Bonds

"And if they be bound in fetters, and be taken in the cords of affliction, then He showeth them their work. . . . He openeth also their ear to instruction. . . ." (Job 36:8–10)

Elihu describes here another aspect of the instruction by suffering. In the first case, the servant of God was placed upon his bed to learn lessons only known through "strong pain." Here he is pictured as *bound and tied* with fetters and cords of affliction—a kingly soul in bonds, learning to endure and to obey so that he may be fitted to reign. Elihu speaks of the soul as "taken" in the cords of affliction, as if this had come suddenly and unawares.

"*Then He showeth them their work.*" The Lord "mighty in strength of heart" flashes His light upon the service of the past, and tenderly shows where His servant has "transgressed" in moving without His commands or "*behaved [himself] proudly*" (36:9) in criticism or harsh judgment of others, in reliance upon his own capabilities, in assurance of his own knowledge, or in thinking himself indispensible to God. Thus the faithful Lord "opens" the "ear" of His children to instruction, and they are taught of Him.

The Way of Deliverance

"He . . . commandeth that they return from iniquity. If they hearken, . . . prosperity and . . . pleasantness. . . . If they hearken not, . . . the sword. . . ." (Job 36:10–12, mg.)

God withdraws His servants from their work to sift and to test it. "He showeth . . . that they have behaved themselves proudly. . . . *He commandeth that they return.*" He convicts only that He may deliver. He rebukes to bless. He wounds that He may heal.

The faithful Lord reveals sin in its true light. *Any shade of pride* is called *iniquity,* and every transgression needs a "return" to God for His pardon and cleansing, as at the very first seeking of Him in early days.

The free choice of the soul is shown in the "*if.*" *If* God's children hearken to His instruction and elect to serve Him alone, seeking nought but His will and pleasure, then they shall again make their way prosperous and have good success. They shall once more find that His commandments are not grievous, that His ways are ways of pleasantness and all His paths are peace.

"*But if they hearken not*"—yes, the soul may turn away from the light, even when the ear has been opened by the Lord and His instruction given. "*If they hearken not,*" the faithful God must use the sword in still sharper dealing; and if His child still fails to listen to His faithful teaching, the end must be a lost life—"saved so as by fire."

Elihu seeks to comfort Job by reminding him that the *godless* in heart do not cry to God for help when they are bound with cords of affliction; they are more often angry (36:13). Therefore Job's very cries to God prove that he is no hypocrite but God's child. But did he not know that God "*delivereth the afflicted by his affliction*" and "*openeth their ear by adversity*" (36:15, mg.)?

Job had been crying to God for deliverance, and God was answering by *leaving him in the furnace,* for the fire would burn all bonds and set him free.

The Purpose of God

> "He would have allured thee out of distress into a broad place." (Job 36:16, mg.)

The soul in the furnace is apt to think the Lord pays no heed to its cry when it is simply unable to discern His silent working. He leads it out of its distress so softly and gently that it is almost unaware of all that He is doing. He is delivering the afflicted by *affliction,* and in adversity the ear is being opened to understand the faintest whisper of the Lord. It knows not that it is being "*allured,*" or silently drawn, out of its fettered position into a "*broad place*" where there is no "*straitness*" of capacity, no narrowness of vision, no smallness of heart, no lack of spiritual food (36:16); for it shall be "abundantly satisfied with the fatness" of His house, and He will spread a table before His freed one in the very presence of its enemies.

The Warning

> "Beware lest thou be allured away by thy sufficiency; neither let the greatness of the Ransom turn thee aside." (Job 36:18, mg.)

Elihu points out to Job that he has been speaking too much of the judgment of the wicked; let him take heed to *himself*, and beware lest *he* is allured from his right place before God by his "*sufficiency*" and drawn aside from keen dealing with sin because of the "*greatness of the Ransom*." All his riches—be they material or spiritual—all the forces of strength would not avail to bring him out of distress (36:19), not even the night of the grave (36:20). The Lord alone could bring him into the broad place.

"*Allured by thy sufficiency*"— this is the danger of every honored servant of God. *Self-sufficiency* at first, and then when this is taken away and the soul has learned to draw upon the sufficiency of God, it is possible for it to be allured from dependence upon Him by the *very sufficiency He has given.*

This is a solemn warning that the "*greatness of the Ransom*" may even be our snare! It seems that we are able only to grasp one aspect at a time of the stupendous sacrifice of Christ and the awful holiness of God, so that we either walk in a measure of bondage—judging our fellowship with God *by our obedience*—or else the *grace of God* and the value of the shed and sprinkled blood of His Son are realized to such an extent that *we fail to deal severely with sin or disobedience* in our daily walk.

The Soul's Choice

> "Take heed, regard not iniquity: for *this hast thou chosen* rather than affliction." (Job 36:21)

Job had "behaved himself proudly" in his self-vindication, and it is described as *iniquity*.

"*Take heed, regard not iniquity,*" Elihu says. "Job, you have chosen it *rather than affliction,* chosen to defend yourself rather than be silent and endure, chosen to take your cause into your own hands."

At every step of the life of faith in God, the soul has a choice before it, and it is always possible to choose the easier path rather than that of affliction. Elihu speaks of the need of guarding the eyes. It is best to *choose unhesitatingly the right course without one glance at any other path,* however lawful it may seem. Many may think this choice an easy matter, but if we were placed in such a crucible as Job was in—what then?

"*Who is a Teacher like unto Him?*" exclaims Elihu (36:22) as he thus unfolds the patient dealing of God with His children and His mighty strength of heart-love toward them. How tenderly God shows them their work, opens their inward ear to understand His instruction, delivers them from their bonds by the fiery trial, and greatly allures them out into the broad place where there is no straitness.

"*Behold, God doeth loftily in His power.*" None can teach Him His way nor charge Him with unrighteousness (36:22–23). Let Job magnify His work and remember that man can only look upon it "*afar off*" (36:24–25), for He is so great that we cannot know Him and understand Him as He is, nor as He was in the far-back ages of eternity (36:26).

The Storm

"Hearken ye unto the noise of His voice, and the muttering that goeth out of His mouth. . . . *God thundereth marvelously with His voice.*" (Job 37:2, 5, mg.)

While Elihu is speaking, a great storm gathers up; and the group upon the ash-mound is wrapped in darkness, broken only by the vivid flashes of lightning.

Elihu knows God, and so his whole being responds with delight to the manifestation of the majesty of Jehovah in *"the storm that cometh up"* (36:33). His words read as if he stood watching the play of the lightning with exultant joy, spontaneously breaking out with the description to the group of men around him.

To Elihu it seems as if Jehovah had come forth in His pavilion, the thunderings betokening His presence as the light spread around His throne (36:29–30). His hands are covered with the lightning, each flash proceeding from Him *"against the assailant"* (36:32, mg.).

Elihu confesses that he trembles in the presence of this mighty Jehovah, but *"Hearken,"* he cries, to *"His voice."* The lightning flashes from His hands to the ends of the earth, and then His glorious voice thunders with majesty (37:2–5). Who can comprehend the workings of a God so marvelous in His power? He speaks to the snow and it falls (37:6); He breathes and the *"ice is given,"* the broad waters are frozen (37:10, mg.); He turns about and guides the clouds filled with lightning (37:11–12). All of this is His doing, whether for "correction" or "mercy" upon His land (37:13).

"Hearken unto this, O Job," continues Elihu; *"Consider the wondrous works of God"* (37:14). Do you know how God causes lightning to obey Him (37:15), how He balances the clouds (37:16), how He quiets the earth with the south wind (37:17, mg.) and spreads out the sky like a molten bronze mirror (37:18)?

"Job, *what shall we say unto Him"*—Jehovah, the Omnipotent One? Shall He be told that we desire to speak to Him? Should we not wish we were swallowed up out of His sight (37:20)? We are not able to look at even the light of the sun, His creation, when it is bright in the skies (37:21).

See, Job, the "*golden splendor*" in the north; what terrible majesty (37:22)! He is "*excellent in power*," yet in plenteous justice He shall not afflict nor do violence to poor finite man (37:23). Men are afraid of Him because they know human wisdom is nought before Him (37:24).

CHAPTER 18

"The Lord hath His way in the whirlwind and in the storm, and the clouds are the dust of His feet." (Nahum 1:3)

THE REVELATION OF GOD TO JOB

"Then the Lord answered Job out of the whirlwind." (Job 38:1)

THE terrific storm has subsided. The thunder has ceased to roar and the lightning to flash in the darkened sky which has been dense as a mirror of cast bronze.

The wind has passed and cleansed the skies. In the north is "golden splendor" so intense and bright that Elihu points to it with the words, *"God hath upon Him terrible majesty"* (37:22).

A hush falls upon the group on the ash-mound as they gaze upon all this sublime beauty, a very glimpse, as it were, of the glory within the veil—even of Him who dwelleth in light unapproachable, King of kings and Lord of lords.

Job had said to Jehovah, *"Call Thou and I will answer,"* and now the Lord will take him at his word. Out of the whirlwind there comes a voice—the voice of God.

Was it but "a sound of gentle stillness," such as the voice which spoke to Elijah?

When Elijah heard it, he "hid his face." Even so must Job have bowed before the Lord.

173

Did his "friends" hear it as well as Job, or did it only penetrate to the inner hearing of his heart? We cannot tell. We only know that Jehovah spoke to His servant and made Himself known to him.

"*Who is this that darkeneth counsel by words without knowledge?*" were the first words that met Job's ear. Job had said that in early days the "counsel of God" had been in his tent, but he is now told that he had "darkened" or brought a veil over that "counsel" by his *multitude of words.*

"*Who is this?*" demands Jehovah. Is *this* My servant whom I called true, upright, blameless, and godly? Job, know thyself. Who are you? What are you after all but a finite man?

The Strengthening of Job

"Gird up now thy loins like a man; . . . answer thou Me." (Job 38:3, A.V.)

Job has been lying upon the ash-mound in mute misery ever since his attempt at self-vindication. Because of "anguish of spirit" he has not been able to respond to the message of deliverance by Elihu; he has been too crushed to answer him one word.

The All-wise Lord knows that a wounded spirit none can raise up but God Himself. He therefore speaks to the stricken Job and bids him gird up his loins like a man.

"Come, Job, rouse yourself, and give Me your attention. Fix your mind upon the questions I ask you, and answer Me" are the words, in effect, addressed to the prostrate man.

No word from the mouth of God is void of power; so we may well believe that the needed strength was conveyed to Job and he was set upon his feet, prepared to hear the voice of God and made ready for the wondrous revelation which the Lord vouchsafed to him.

Even thus did the Lord deal with His servant Ezekiel when he fell upon his face at the vision of the Man upon the throne. "*Stand upon thy feet, and I will speak with thee,*" said Jehovah, and *with the word* the Spirit entered into him and set him upon his feet, strengthened to bear the interview with the Eternal God.

Again, it is written of Daniel that his face was set toward the ground in mute helplessness before the Man with the eyes of fire who spoke to him, and he was not able to listen to His voice until the hand touched him, when he said, "*Let my Lord speak; for Thou hast strengthened me.*"

The Lord does not repeat to the now strengthened Job the message sent him by the mouth of Elihu. The way of deliverance through the Ransom has been told him; the interpretation of God's dealings with him has been given. *It is not further teaching that Job needs but a direct interview with God*—such a revelation of Jehovah as will bring him to the dust and give him a glimpse into the heart of Him who has placed him in the crucible.

The Voice from the Throne

"*Where* wast thou? . . . *Hast* thou? . . . *Canst* thou? . . . *Knowest* thou? . . . *Wilt* thou?" (Job 38:4, 12, 31, 33, 39)

Having strengthened Job to hear His words, the Lord addresses him with direct questions as, in beauty of language that has no parallel, He outlines before him in brief and vivid word-pictures His mighty power in heaven and upon earth, making His glory to pass before the eyes of His servant even as He did to Moses when He proclaimed before him "a God full of compassion and gracious, . . . plenteous in mercy and truth."

"WHERE WAST THOU *when I laid the foundations of the earth?*" (38:4)

The Lord's first words put Job into his right place as a creature before his Creator.

Job had said to Zophar, "*I have understanding as well as you,*" when he resented being taught by his friends what he felt he knew even better than they; but his wisdom is quickly brought to nought by the first question of Jehovah.

If he had "understanding," let him declare to his Creator the mystery of his own being. Where was he at the time of the creation of the earth? Who had determined its measures? Could he tell whereon its foundations were fastened? Did he know who laid the cornerstone of it in the midst of all the company of heaven?

If Job's wisdom was not able to fathom these things, how could he understand the mystery of his own creation and as a finite creature fathom the dealings of God with him?

"WHO *shut up the sea with doors, . . . prescribed for it My boundary, . . . and said, . . . NO further?*" (38:8–11, mg.)

If Jehovah had shut up the mighty sea within the boundary of His will and was able to say to the foaming waters, "*Here shall thy proud waves be stayed,*" had not the same Lord supreme control over the swelling of Jordan? Had He not prescribed the boundary line for Job's sorrows, and could He not say "*No further*" to the rabble of evildoers who, Job had complained, were overwhelming him "as a wide breaking in of waters"?

"HAST THOU *commanded the morning, . . . caused the dayspring to . . . take hold of . . . the earth, and the wicked be shaken out of it . . . and . . . broken?*" (38:12–15)

If Jehovah could clothe the earth with light by the

breaking forth of the morning so that it is changed as clay takes the impress of the seal (38:14), could He not as rapidly speak the word and bring forth His servant out of his darkness into the light of the resurrection day? Could He not cause the light to "take hold" of him so that the wicked hosts around him should be dispersed with their power broken and his life changed and marked with the impress of God as clay under a seal?

> "HAST THOU *entered into the springs of the sea* [*and*] *the recesses of the deep? . . . Hast thou seen the gates of the shadow of death?*" (38:16–17)

If Job could not see the springs of the mighty ocean nor have access to the recesses of the deep; if he could not discern the shadows of death nor perceive the gates, or turning-point, between life and death; if not, how could he understand the springs within his own being and know the recesses of his own heart? He had talked of drawing near to the land of the shadow of death, but those had been words without knowledge. Jehovah alone could deal with the springs of life, lay bare the recesses of the deep of his being, and control the gates of death.

> "HAST THOU *comprehended the breadth of the earth,* . . . *the way to the dwelling of light* [*and the*] *darkness?*" (38:18–19)

"Doubtless thou knowest!" said Jehovah to His listening servant, gently pressing upon him with loving irony the folly of questioning the actions of such a God. If Job could not discern the paths of light and darkness (38:19–20), how could he comprehend the way in which he himself should be led to Him who is the *dwelling* of light to all of His redeemed?

> "HAST THOU *entered the treasuries of the snow* [*and*] *the hail . . . reserved against the time of trouble, against the day of battle and war?*" (38:22–23)

Did Job know the resources of Jehovah? He had

said that this was a warfare appointed to man upon the earth, but did he understand anything of the conflict in the unseen realms and know the forces reserved by the Lord as a man of war *against the day of battle?*

The words of the Lord give a glimpse into a conflict in the unseen realms which has lasted for ages and of which *the climax* is shown *only when the veil is lifted* in the book of Revelation, when the "war in heaven" between Michael and his angels and the devil with his hosts of darkness is disclosed.

The stormy wind, the "flame of a devouring fire" with crashing and tempest and hailstones—these are spoken of in other parts of Scripture as used by the Lord in the day of battle; and Daniel speaks of a *"time of trouble, such as never was"* coming upon the earth. At that time it shall be said, "The Lord hath opened His armory, and hath brought forth the weapons of His indignation."

Did Job not know that Jehovah had infinite resources for aiding him in the warfare appointed to him? Surely He was better able to deal with the "indictment" written against Job by his prosecutor than Job himself!

> "Who *hath cleft a channel for the waterflood?"* Who parts the rays of light, controls the east wind, directs the way of the lightning, commands the rain to fall upon the desolate land to satisfy its needs, and causes the tender grass to spring forth? From what source comes the rain, the drops of dew, the ice, the hoary frost of heaven, and the waters hardened like rock when the surface of the deep is frozen? (38:24–30)

If Jehovah commands the forces of nature and directs the wind and rain to fulfill each its part in meeting the thirst of the earth, causing the tender green grass to spring forth to cover it with beauty, surely the same Lord controls all the forces around His servant Job so that, in the end, his need will be

...sfied and his life spring forth again in power.

"CANST THOU" *bind, loose, lead forth, and guide the stars in their courses? Canst thou establish the ordinances of the heavens, command the clouds, send forth lightning, put wisdom in the dark clouds, give understanding to the meteor, number the clouds, and pour out the bottles of heaven until the clods of earth cling together* (38:31–38, mg.)

It was well that Job had been strengthened by the empowering word of Jehovah before He spoke with him further, for the mind of finite man might well be overwhelmed with the majesty of the themes and the rapidly outlined pictures of the All-powerful Lord: the *earth* founded in space, the *restless ocean* shut in within the boundary of His will, the *dayspring* clothing the earth as a garment, the *recesses of the deep* laid before His eyes, the *knowledge* of the mysterious gates of death, the *resources* in the treasuries of hail and snow, the *control* of waterflood, wind, and rain, the *breathing upon the waters* for the formation of frost and ice, and the *leading and guiding* of the planets of heaven as if they were but trifles in His hand.

None but the Sovereign Lord of heaven and earth could thus summarize with masterly ease the forces at His command and point to light and darkness, wind and rain, hail and snow, as a master workman points to the instruments with which he fulfills his will.

"WILT THOU . . . *satisfy the appetite of the young lions? Who provideth for the raven his food when his young ones cry unto God?"* (38:39–41)

Let Job turn from the starry heavens, so vast and wonderful, and think even of the animal creation. Who provides for their needs? Did Jehovah create them and *then neglect them*? He had placed in them their instincts and their appetites; and when the young ravens cried for food, it was a *cry to God,* and their Creator was not oblivious of their need.

If the Lord thus watched over His lower creation, surely He would not fail to heed the cry of His servant Job. The desire of his soul for God would certainly be satisfied. Did Job not know that it was *the instinct of all creatures to provide for the need of their young*? How much more does the great Father-heart of God respond to the soul that has its life from Himself, saying, "*I* have made, and *I* will bear; even *I* will carry and deliver you."

"KNOWEST THOU *the time when the wild goats . . . bring forth? . . . Canst thou number the months that they fulfill?*" (39:1–4)

It is written that it is not for man to know times and seasons which the Father has set within His own authority. Even so the *moment* of birth and death for man and beast knoweth no man, but the Father only.

Job had cried for deliverance from the trial he was in, but Jehovah alone knew the *hour* when his warfare would be accomplished, the *moment* when his sorrows would be over and he would emerge once more into the light of God.

"WHO *hath sent out the wild ass free,*" loosed his bands so that he scorns the tumult of the city? He is deaf to the voice of the taskmaster and his range is the mountains. Will these free creatures be slaves? Will they obey any voice but Mine? Can they be bound or made to follow after man? (39:5–12)

What glorious freedom is given to the wild creatures whose range is the mountains! They are free by the instincts of the life within them and cannot be bound by the will of men.

"Even so, Job, will *I loose you from your bonds* and bring you out of the furnace into a fuller life in union with Myself—when your service to Me shall again be the glad, spontaneous outcome of that life within. Your range shall be upon the mountains, your pasture shall be found in the mount of God; you shall be free indeed."

*   *   *

The sympathy of Jehovah with the work of His hands in the animal creation is shown in His response to their cry for food, His noting of their sorrows in the hour of travail, and His pleasure in the freedom of the wild creatures He has made.

The Lord will show Job yet other examples of His workmanship that he might not fail to understand the infinite resources and wisdom of God.

The Ostrich

"God hath deprived her of wisdom [yet] what time she rouseth herself up to flight, she scorneth the horse and his rider." (39:13–18, mg.)

The Horse

"Hast thou given the horse his might? . . . He rejoiceth in his strength. . . . He mocketh at fear, and is not dismayed. . . . He swalloweth the ground with fierceness and rage." (39:19–24)

The Hawk and the Eagle

"Doth the hawk soar by thy wisdom? . . . Doth the eagle mount up at thy command, and make her nest on high?" (39:26–27)

Let Job ponder over the workmanship of God in these creatures, each fitted for its own sphere and to fulfill the purpose of its creation.

The *same creative hand* made ostrich, horse, and eagle, and the *same life* moves in each, yet differs in manifestation; each acts by the spontaneous movement and instinct of its being to fulfill the purpose of God.

The *ostrich* has not been endowed with wisdom, yet when she takes to flight she excels in speed.

The *horse* has not the speed of the ostrich, yet see

his force and strength in battle as he rejoices in the sound of the trumpet and shouts of war.

The *eagle* mounts up to heaven above every other bird. Mark her piercing vision as she spies her prey afar off and seeks it as food for her young.

Did Job not understand that he, too, was but a unit in the great creation of God, with only a *measure of knowledge and power* imparted to him to fulfill the purpose of his creation.

Where is thy wisdom, Job, compared with Mine?

The Lord's Question

"Shall he that *contendeth with the Almighty instruct Him*?" (A.V.) "He that argueth with God, let him answer. . . ." (40:2)

The Lord waits for Job to answer all these things, for Job had said that he was prepared to reason with the Lord over His strange dealings with him. But did Job *still* think he could instruct his Creator how to fashion the work of His hands?

Job had protested that he would fill his mouth with arguments if he could but get access to the throne of Jehovah; *let him therefore speak.*

Job's First Question

"Then Job answered . . . and said, Behold, I am of small account; what shall I answer thee? I lay mine hand upon my mouth. . . . I will proceed no further." (40:3–5)

"*I am vile*" (A.V.), cries Job, "*contemptibly mean*" (as the word signifies), and of small account.

What answer could Job give to the God he has misjudged? What could he say to such a revelation of His power, His infinite wisdom, and His sympathy with the work of His hands?

Job feels contemptibly mean as he remembers his language toward the Lord and how he charged Him with cruel persecution when He was but working out His purposes of love.

Job replies to Jehovah's challenge by admitting that he can only place his hand over his mouth and confess himself silenced. He will not speak any more as he has done.

Job is *silenced,* it is true. Even so, the Lord must have from him a more frank confession of repentance and a deeper turning from himself and the past than this contrite response!

CHAPTER 19

"It was too painful for me; until I went into the sanctuary of God. [Then] my soul was grieved, and I was pricked in my heart: so brutish am I, and ignorant; I was as a beast before Thee." (Psalm 73:16, 21–22, mg.)

JOB THE VANQUISHED

"The Lord . . . said, Gird up thy loins now like a man: I will demand of thee. . . . *Wilt thou condemn Me,* that thou mayest be justified?" (Job 40:6–8)

THE voice out of the whirlwind addresses Job once more. He is bidden again to "*gird up his loins*" ("stand up like a man," we would say) and prepare to answer the questions put to him. Let him declare his attitude to God. Was he determined to *condemn* his Creator to *justify himself*? Would he even "*disannul His judgments*" (v. 8), rendering void all His patient dealings with him in the crucible, by refusing to take the place of repentance at His feet?

Was he going to declare in the face of all God's working in creation that he had been dealt with more severely than the very beasts of the field?

The Omniscient Lord saw that *Job had not yet ceased from clinging to his personal integrity.* Yes, he had admitted that he was of little account. He owned that he felt humbled and contemptibly mean before the majesty of Jehovah, for he could neither control the stars, feed the wild creatures, nor give to the horse and the eagle their strength and power of flight. He had also confessed that he ought not to

185

have spoken as he had done, and would proceed no
further in such folly.

However, the Lord sees that He must deal more
personally with Job to bring him to the dust. He had
reminded him of His power in creation, and Job had
only been silenced before the greatness of his God;
now he must be reminded that *none of the power he
had earlier had over others had been his own. He
must* learn in deeper measure his own helplessness.

> "HAST THOU *an arm like God? And canst thou thunder
> with a voice like Him? Deck thyself now with excel-
> lency and dignity, and array thyself with honor and
> majesty. . . . Look upon every one that is proud . . . and
> bring him low; and tread down the wicked . . . in the
> dust.*" (40:9–13)

If you can do *these* things, Job, then will I admit
that you are able to save yourself (40:14), speaks
Jehovah to the silenced man at His feet.

Job had said that in the days of old he had sat as
chief in the midst of the people, clothed with righteousness and diademed with justice. He had spoken
of his power to pluck the prey of the wicked from
their teeth, and of the way in which others had been
silenced by his words.

Jehovah's question presses close to home, for Job
knew that all this authority and power had been
stripped from him. He is painfully aware that *he can
no more reclothe himself with it* than he can array
himself in the majesty of God. That *of himself* he was
unable to humble his fellow men had been proved in
his failure to convince his friends, and that he could
not *save* himself was manifested in the complete
uselessness of his self-vindication.

Job has no answer to give to this last question of
Jehovah—no more than to the others; but the home-
thrust has now reached him and touched him in the

vital point of his despair.

The Lord is touching the quick now, and slowly bringing His servant down to the place of emptiness and blessing.

Jehovah's Picture Lesson

"Behold now behemoth." (40:15)

Once more the Lord points to His wonders in creation and describes to Job two huge creatures called "behemoth"* and "leviathan."

Jehovah calls behemoth *the chief of the ways of God"* (40:19). His *strength,* his *force* (40:16), his *sinews* (40:17), his *bones* like tubes of brass, his *limbs* like bars of iron (40:18) are all minutely described. *"He only that made him* can approach him with His sword" (40:19), the Lord says, and this may be the point Job needs to be taught.

None but the Creator can deal with the creature, and *only God can humble the proud* and bring low the haughtiness of man. Only in Jehovah the Lord was there salvation for Job in his need.

One other lesson for Job there might be in the calm confidence of the huge "behemoth." The creature could watch a river violently overflow without trembling, and he remained confident though *"Jordan swell even to his mouth"* (40:23), for he knew that he would not sink. The very instinct of his life told him that the swelling waters would but carry him wherever he would go.

Did Job not understand that in the deep waters of trial he had been passing through—when the waves and billows had appeared to swallow him up—did he not *know* that he could not sink? The Spirit of God

---

* "The hippopotamus," R.V. margin; "the elephant," A.V. margin. Another possibility is "the dinosaur."

had breathed *life* into him, and the waters could not overflow him but would bear him ever nearer to his God.

Jehovah's Second Object Lesson

"Canst thou draw out leviathan with a fish hook?"
(41:1)

Jehovah's second picture lesson is another huge creature called "leviathan."*

Still more minutely does the Lord describe this powerful creature and the impossibility of his being tamed by man.

No human being could put a rope through his nostril (41:2). None could play with him or *tame him* to be their servant or pet (41:4–5). The merchants could not make use of him for merchandise (41:6). None *dare lay his hand upon him* (41:8) or venture to stir him up (41:10). Men are cast down at the sight of him (41:9). His limbs, his mighty strength, his terrible teeth, his scales, his eyes, his mouth, his nostrils, his breath like sparks of fire, make him so terrible that *the strongest men fear him* (41:12–25). No weapon avails to touch him, for he *"counteth iron as straw, and brass as rotten wood"* (41:26–29). As he rushes through the watery depths, it boils and leaves a shining wake behind him. *"Upon earth there is not his like"* in absolute fearlessness; he is *"king over all the sons of pride"* (41:34)!

"Who then is he that can stand before Me?" questions Jehovah of His waiting servant. If men are cast down at the sight of the creature, *will they not fear before his Creator?*

Jehovah's Final Claim

"Who hath first given unto Me, that I should repay

---

* "The crocodile," R.V. margin; "the whale," A.V. margin.

him? Whatsoever is under the whole heaven is *Mine*."
(41:11)

This is the conclusion of the whole matter and the
climax of the Lord's dealing with Job.

Job had said that Jehovah had taken away his
rights, but the Lord declares that Job has no rights!
As Sovereign Lord of heaven and earth, Jehovah is
under no obligation to any creature. None can demand anything of Him as a *right*. On the contrary,
they must acknowledge His claim! "MINE" is written
by Him upon all things, animate and inanimate,
under the whole heaven.

Job, "*Behold now behemoth, which I made with
thee*." Behemoth is Mine, and *you are Mine*. I have
the sovereign right of doing what I will with Mine
own.

AND JOB IS VANQUISHED!

Job's Submission

> "Then Job answered the Lord, and said, I know that
> Thou canst do everything, and that no thought of Thine
> can be hindered." (42:1–2, mg.)

In Job's first answer to the Lord he confessed that
he felt contemptibly mean, as he remembered his
words of reproach against Him whose heart was now
revealed to him as tenderly sympathetic even with
the lower creation—and much more with His creature man, upon whom He had set His love and sought
to "visit" or have communion with every moment.

Job bows before the claim of his Creator and cries,
"*I know* that Thou canst do everything." In complete
surrender and with the worship of his whole being,
he acknowledges anew the sovereign power of God
and, with renewed faith, gives Him His right place in
his life.

"No thought of Thine can be hindered" is the confession of the vanquished Job. He had *believed* it and even *said* it to the friends in one of his moments of tenacious trust in God, but now he *knows* it with a "full assurance of understanding" never realized before. He sees that all his cries and writhings in the crucible had not hindered the Lord from revealing Himself to him in the fullness of time, not even his fainting under his sufferings or his pleadings to Him to *"let him alone."*

The immutable Lord had waited until the furnace had fulfilled His purpose; nor had He interposed in answer to Job's cries of pain, because He knew that his *will* would remain true to Him to the very end.

"I know that no purpose of Thine can be restrained," Job answers the Lord. He looks back upon his past months of suffering and in the light of Jehovah's presence sees the purpose of love behind it all.

Not one hard word from his well-intentioned friends, not one pang of pain, not one weary night or sorrowful day could have come to him but by the express permission of his faithful Lord.

Again the Lord appears to speak to Job in the words: *"Who is this that hideth counsel without knowledge?"* (42:3).

Had Job learned his lesson? He had bowed before the Lord and acknowledged His sovereign power and claim upon him as his Creator, but did Job confess his ignorance and own that he had veiled the counsel of God by his words without knowledge?

Job's Confession of Ignorance

> ". . . I uttered that which I understood not, *things too wonderful for me,* which *I knew not."* (42:3)

Job replies to the Lord that he unreservedly acknowledges that he has uttered words he did not really understand. He admits that he had talked of things "too wonderful" for his finite mind to grasp (see Psalm 139:5–6).

He had said to Zophar, "I am not inferior to you; what ye know, the same do I know also." But he sees now that he was not willing to be *thought ignorant by his friends,* and much less was he willing to be taught by them what *they* considered they knew of God.

Job remembers how he had actually been tempted to show his would-be teachers that he knew as much as they (27:11)! It was all bitterly true; he sees that he could take the dust before *the Lord* and worship *Him* when blow after blow fell upon him, but he could not take the low place before his *friends* and allow *them* to treat him as an ignorant, presumptuous man, much less as a hypocrite and a secret transgressor against the Lord.

In his heart Job had honestly desired to be humble and show no pride of position to his servants (31:13–15) or his friends, but it was one thing to be humble in that way and another to be willing to be considered ignorant of the things of God by those whose knowledge of Him was less than his own.

Now Job understands Elihu's words about the Lord withdrawing His children from their work to "*hide pride*" from them and to save them from greater sorrow in the world to come.

In shame Job looks up to the Lord. *Will You let me once more speak,* he humbly requests (42:4).

The Lord appears to answer Job with the very words He had spoken to him at the beginning of the interview (40:7). Jehovah is now "demanding" of Job the confession of his attitude to Him; let him therefore "*declare unto Him*" what he has to say (42:4).

Job's Verdict on His Past

"I had heard of Thee by the hearing of the ear; but

now mine eye seeth Thee." (42:5)

Very wonderful are the glimpses into the heart of God given us in His dealings with Job. So precious to the Lord are His servants who walk with Him in integrity of heart that He yearns for their complete understanding and accord with Him in all His dealings with them and His people in general.

"Ye shall be *comforted* concerning the evil that I have brought upon Jerusalem, . . . and ye shall *know that I have not done in vain* all that I have done in it" was the Lord's word to His servant Ezekiel when telling him of all the sore judgments He would send upon Israel. In like manner the Lord desires that Job should acknowledge that He has dealt rightly with him; so He reveals His heart to him and then waits until Job passes judgment upon himself and his past.

"Declare thou unto Me" (42:4), said Jehovah, and Job responds. *I thought I knew Thee, Lord, for Thou wert with me in the days of old. Thy Spirit was upon me. I called upon Thee, and Thou didst answer and bless me on every side, but now that mine eye seeth Thee* I know that my past knowledge of Thee was, as it were, a *"hearing of the ear."* My inner ears were opened to Thine instruction, but *the eyes of my heart have never beheld Thee until now!*

We should pause here to consider the significance of what God has revealed to Job.

We have now seen that the Book of Job is thought to be the oldest book extant, older than the records of Genesis and the books of Moses. Surely the Divine Spirit must have had a very special purpose in its preservation.

May it not be that it contains the account of the first and primary revelation of God to His fallen creatures, to be followed in successive years by a

gradual unveiling of Himself—from the center out-
wards, so to speak—drawing nearer and nearer to
man until in the fullness of time He was manifested
in His Son, Christ Jesus, through whom His banished ones might return to their Creator and in re-
creation become sons of God.

To Job the Lord is revealed as the great First
Cause, the central spring or pivot, so to say, of all
creation—the One who directs and moves all things
from His throne.

Elijah, trained by God Himself in the mountains of
Gilead, was given the same knowledge of Jehovah so
that he was able in unshaken faith to ask that there
would be no rain on the land of Israel for three years.
He knew the God upon the throne of the universe, the
One who declared to Job that He had treasures of
snow and hail reserved for the day of battle.

To the redeemed today, the same God is revealed in
His Son Jesus Christ. Paul wrote of Christ that He
was the image of the invisible God, declaring that *in
Him* were all things created, . . . and *in Him all things
hold together* (Colossians 1:16–17, mg.), thus making
Him equal with God—Creator as well as Redeemer.

It is the joy of the Son to reveal the Father to His
redeemed. In union with Him—and especially as they
walk with Him, beholding with *unveiled face* the glory
of the Lord—they are led by the Lord the Spirit from
glory to glory, ever nearer and nearer to Him who sits
upon the throne—until they, too, know God as He
was revealed to Job. And *from the inner sanctuary of
God's presence they look out upon the universe,* seeing how His voice moves the waters, breaks the ce-
dars, spits out flames of fire, shakes the wilderness,
and strips the forest bare (Psalm 29), while in the
sanctuary of His immediate presence the seraphim
cry, "Holy, Holy, Holy, is the Lord of Hosts: *the whole
earth is full of His glory*" (Isaiah 6:3).

The story of Job teaches us that this innermost knowledge of God is given only when the soul has been stripped of all that may even unknowingly dim its inner vision and keep it preoccupied—absorbed with its *blessings* instead of with *God*, or with the *work* rather than the *will* of God.

The wondrous gifts of God and our present knowledge about the Lord *may easily keep us from the deepest knowledge of God Himself.*

In Job we clearly observe the contrast between the possession of gifts—which so often tend to build us up in ourselves and make us think we know more than others—and the necessary stripping of all we thought we possessed so that, having nothing, we may truly possess *all things in Him* who is the Source and Possessor of all.

"*I had heard of Thee, but now mine eyes seeth Thee,*" cries Job, as he looks back upon the past which he had considered the "ripeness of his days." "*I have uttered that which I understood not, things too wonderful for me,*" is his verdict upon the knowledge he had thought so great!

Job *knows himself and his measure* at last. He is becoming the little child that Elihu had described: content to lie upon its Father's heart, to know all that the Father wishes it to know, and no more—content to be simply what the Father wishes it to be, while it rejoices with true gladness in the gifts and graces vouchsafed to others in the Father's house.

Job's Self-Loathing

"Now mine eye seeth Thee, wherefore I abhor myself, and repent in dust and ashes." (42:5–6)

"*I abhor myself*" and "*loathe my words*" (42:6, mg.), cries Job. The light of God has given to him the same knowledge of himself as was given in later years to

Isaiah the prophet, when he saw the Lord high and lifted up and cried, "*I am a man of unclean lips.*"

Job had said to Eliphaz that the speeches of one who was desperate were only for the wind and should not be taken seriously (6:26). Now Job sees that superfluity of speech must be *renounced* if he is to walk in fellowship with God. The "precious" must be taken from the "vile"; that which is "*true [gold] must be separated from the dross*" if he is to be once more a messenger of God (Jeremiah 15:19, Swedish translation).

It is significant that the Apostle James places "*stumbling not in word*" as the supreme mark of a man fully under the control of God. The same man, James says, is able to bridle the whole body (3:2).

The reference to *Job* by the Apostle James (5:11) shows that he had studied his history and may have had him in mind earlier as he pressed home his message of "patience" to the tried ones of his day, beseeching them to "*count it joy*" when in manifold trials, for the "*proof of their faith*" would work patience, and patience must needs have its perfect work if they were to be perfect and entire, lacking nothing. James well knew that the patience of Christ could only be wrought into a person's character by the fire of trial.

"*I loathe my words,*" cries Job as he sees that he should have suffered in silence and have left his vindication to his God. Does he recognize *now* that the very *expression* of his sorrows had magnified them in his own eyes? Does he realize *now* how the multitude of words wasted his strength and made him so much the less able to endure that he had fainted under the hand of God?

In any case, he loathes *himself* and his *words* as having come *from himself,* for the tongue had "set on fire" the wheel of birth, the life of nature (James 3:6, mg.). It is set on fire, James says, by the powers of darkness, possibly recalling the injunction of the Lord: "Let your speech be, Yea, yea; Nay, nay: and *whatsoever is more than these is of the evil one*" (Matthew 5:37).

As the searchlight of God is thrown upon his past, Job remembers those words of gloomy despair and longing for death, of sarcastic contempt for Zophar, of bitter reasoning to Bildad, of petulant crying and pleading with God to leave him alone. What if He had taken him at his word! And then the words describing the way that God had used him to others—*how could he thus have spoken of himself?*

Job thinks of the way he was offended with Jehovah and how he had reproached Him with *cruelty* after walking with Him so loyally in the past. He remembers his miserable collapse upon the ash-heap and his pitiful attempt to clear his own character to his misjudging friends.

"*I abhor myself*" and "*loathe my words*" is the only language of Job's heart in the light of all that God has revealed. *He can say no more about his past integrity.* He will not ask again for the restoration of past blessings, for now he sees that he did not know himself nor understand his need.

CHAPTER 20

"We went through fire and through water; but Thou broughtest us out into abundance." (Psalm 66:12, mg.)

JOB'S CAPTIVITY TURNED

"It was so, that after the Lord had spoken . . . unto Job, the Lord said to Eliphaz. . . ." (Job 42:7)

THE Lord has brought Job into his right place before Him, so He now turns to Eliphaz and his two friends.

Job had confidently declared that his Redeemer would vindicate him in the day of His coming to judge the earth—sometime in the distant future—but Jehovah cannot allow His servant to remain under the misjudgment of his fellows, so He will vindicate him *at once* and "bring forth his righteousness as the light, and his judgment as the noonday."

"*My wrath is kindled against thee, and against thy two friends*" (42:7), said Jehovah to Eliphaz, singling him out by name for special reproof because *he* of all the three had assumed spiritual authority and most emphatically asserted that his knowledge had been obtained directly from God!

Eliphaz had repeated to Job what he heard from the spirit-form, but Jehovah repudiates the teaching of the spirit-voice by saying to Eliphaz, "*Ye have not spoken of Me the thing that is right . . .*" (42:8).

These words make it still more manifest that the vision Eliphaz had described to Job was not from God, but from the Adversary who had set his heart

197

upon causing Job to renounce his faith in God.

In these last most-perilous times, lying spirits are again sent forth from the pit to "show great signs and wonders; so as to *lead astray,* if possible, even the elect" (Matthew 24:24; compare with 2 Thessalonians 2:9). May God grant that His children refuse to give heed to all the subtle voices of spirit-forms, remembering that "God, having of old time spoken unto the fathers . . . in divers manners, *hath at the end of these days spoken unto us in His Son"* (Hebrews 1:1-2) and by the Holy Spirit, who will teach us how to abide in Him and instruct us also how to "*prove the spirits, whether they be of God."*

"Ye have not spoken of Me the thing that is right, *as My servant Job hath,"* said the Lord to Bildad and Zophar as well as to Eliphaz, thus rejecting not only the words of the lying spirit to Eliphaz but *all* the ideas of suffering expressed by the three men.

The Lord moreover emphatically declared that Job had said of Him *"the thing that was right"* in saying that *the hand of God had touched him,* and that He was but dealing with him as assayers deal with true gold—placing it in a crucible of fire for the removal of the dross.

We therefore see clearly from the words of Jehovah that the children of God must *refuse to dwell on the second causes* in their lives. The Adversary may attack them as he attacked Job, but only by express permission from God! They need not be *occupied with watching for the Adversary* in all that comes to them, but in all and through all should recognize the hand of *God,* even as the Lord Jesus did when He said, "The cup which the *Father* hath given Me, shall I not drink it?" at the very time He calls *"the hour and the power of darkness."*

The story of Job comes with fresh power in these days when the enemy is coming in like a flood, having great wrath, knowing that his time is short. It should remind the redeemed that in their triumphant Lord they are given *"power over all the power of the enemy"*—as they look beyond all second causes, be they satanic or human, to Him who sits on the heavenly throne. For "the Lord sat as King at the flood; yea the Lord sitteth as King for ever" (Psalm 29:10–11). The child of God must shelter under the power of the living Christ and abide in the keeping of the Father, leaving to *Him* the stilling of the enemy and the avenger (Psalm 8:2).

"Ye have not spoken of Me the thing that is right," declares Jehovah to the three men. They had said that God was angry with His servant Job and was punishing him for transgression, yet it was afterwards proved that God was but leading him on to a fuller knowledge of Himself and breaking him down on every side to make room for the reception of the divine abundance.

"Ye have not spoken of Me the thing that is right, as *My servant Job* hath," said Jehovah, thus confessing Job before his friends, even as He had done before the council of heaven, *to be His servant.* He was not ashamed to be called his God!

"My servant Job!"—so Jehovah graciously acknowledges the man who had become the open abhorring of outcasts and friends, and had drunk, in his measure, the cup of sorrow to the dregs.

The Command to the Friends

"*Go to My servant Job,* and offer up for yourselves a burnt offering, and *My servant Job* shall pray for you." (Job 42:8)

"Seven bullocks and seven rams" were the rebuked men to take and offer to God as a confession of sin and an acknowledgment that their guilt could only be atoned for by the shedding of blood—the number seven indicating the need of a full and complete sacrifice before they could be forgiven.

Moreover, they had to humble themselves and accord with Jehovah's estimation of Job by *going to him* so that *he* might pray for them, thus admitting they had wronged him.

It was true that they had not known the Lord to the degree Job had. They were clearly well-intentioned in their desire to help him, however; yet the Lord's severe rebuke shows that He considered them guilty of hardness to their brother in affliction. Jehovah plainly tells them that only for Job's sake and by humbling themselves to him can they escape His severe dealing for their foolish, short-sighted judgment of a man whose character should have commanded trust—even when they did not understand his path—and for their self-complacent assumption of knowledge of the ways of God.

Are you crying to the Lord to avenge His own elect? Wait *His* time! Hear now this, afflicted one: "Thus saith thy Lord the LORD . . . Behold, I have taken out of thine hand the cup of staggering, . . . thou shalt no more drink it again; and I will put it into the hand of them that afflict thee, which have said to thy soul, Bow down, that we may go over: and thou hast laid thy back . . . as the street, to them that go over" (Isaiah 51:22–23).

Jehovah's dealing with Job and his friends has been repeated again and again in the history of the children of God. We may point to Joseph and his brothers as an example in detail, and remember how the brothers who had despitefully used him had eventually to bow themselves down before him and receive bread from his hands. Joseph, of course, foreshadows the Christ Himself, who was rejected and yet to whom eventually *every* knee shall bow.

The principles of God's dealings with man are as unchanging as the immutable God Himself. "*God resisteth the proud, but giveth grace to the humble*" (James 4:6). "Whosoever shall *exalt himself* shall be *humbled*, and whosoever shall *humble himself* shall be *exalted*" (Matthew 23:12).

"*My servant Job shall pray for you, for him will I accept*" (42:8), said Jehovah to the men who had told Job that God was exacting less of him than his iniquity deserved!

And Eliphaz, Bildad and Zophar "did according as the Lord commanded them," and "*He pardoned their sin for the sake of Job*" (42:9, Septuagint version).

Job's Deliverance

"And the Lord turned the captivity of Job, *when* he prayed for his friends. . . ." (42:10)

It is not written that the Lord turned the captivity of Job and *then* he prayed for his friends, but that *when* he prayed for them his own release came!

Jehovah had revealed Himself to Job, rebuked his would-be helpers, and acknowledged him as His servant. But outwardly Job was still an afflicted man, bereft of all he had once possessed: homeless, friendless, a "*beggar upon the dunghill*."

Surely Job's need was prayer for himself first; *he* must be delivered before he can pray for others. But *No!* Jehovah had instructed the three men to go to the outcast upon the ash-mound, who would then pray for them, and the Lord would accept his prayer.

The Lord said nothing to Job about *deliverance for himself*, but He did say He would *accept* him as he prayed for his accusers. Job must therefore put aside all thought about his present condition and cooperate with the *known will of God*. He must not wait for outward and manifest deliverance from his sorrows, but must cease from himself and *his* affairs and attend to the needs of his friends.

As the three men come to him, still a broken man, did Job think in his heart, "Are my would-be comforters, who have condemned me and dealt so severely with me, to be thought of *first?* Are *they* to be pardoned and blessed while I, whom God has acknowledged to be His servant, am not to be thought of *at all? Is there no deliverance for me?*"

The three men come to Job, and while outwardly a beggar, he acts like a prince! The Lord had *said* that He would accept him, so he rests upon the word of the living God and acts *as a prince* of the heavenly realm—*a prince having power with God!*

Job *prays for his friends.* What a test of his inner spirit! He must pray with *desire,* or his prayer would be in vain. Does he really, with his *whole soul,* desire that the men who had misjudged him so cruelly and dealt with him so hardly should be forgiven and blessed while he is left apparently *undelivered* upon the ash-mound outside the village?

Yes, Job was able to pray in such a way that he prevailed with God, and he asked the blessing for others that *he could not ask for himself!* Even as the Lord Jesus prayed in the midst of His own suffering for those who crucified Him, so was Job's prayer.

The *spirit* of the crucified Jesus is thus seen to be manifested in Job, even as he trod, in wondrous foreshadowing of the Master's footsteps, the pathway of the cross.

Job *prays,* and *as* he prays the word of power is spoken from the throne: "*Deliver him. . . . I have found a Ransom.*" The kingly soul in the bonds of affliction is set free, his captivity is turned, and the days of his mourning are ended.

Nothing is said of the *way* in which Job's captivity was turned! The immediate results of the word of deliverance are not told us, possibly because they are of little importance in the eyes of the Lord who looks upon the heart. Possibly also because the All-wise Lord knew how His children in the furnace of trial would be tempted to set their minds upon the outward and visible signs of blessing, rather than the inward and spiritual grace so much greater in value to Him.

It is sufficient for us to know that the turning point of Job's pathway of trial came *when he entirely ceased from himself* and prayed for his friends.

If you are in the crucible of trial, then learn this lesson: You have been stripped of all your past strength and power; you have writhed and agonized for deliverance from the bonds of affliction; you have had the light of God upon you, and now are loathing yourself and wondering when deliverance will come. Do you not see in the object lesson before you that your captivity shall be turned *when you turn from yourself* and *leave yourself* in the hand of God? When you cease to think of your own needs, and in your emptiness and poverty *give yourself to the ministry for others,* caring nothing at all for yourself? When you desire with your whole heart *the blessing of others more than your own,* and rest content with the will of God, whether it be deliverance from the furnace or *no deliverance,* so that you may have a better resurrection and shine as a brighter jewel in the Master's crown?

A Double Portion

"And the Lord gave Job *twice as much as he had before.*" (42:10)

Thus briefly are we again given a glimpse into the heart of God and shown His purpose in placing His loved ones in the crucible. Jehovah gives back to Job more than He had taken away; yea, He added "*unto the double*" (see Isaiah 61:7).

The "*double*" given to Job at this point of his spiritual history is strikingly explained by other passages of Scripture:

In the statutes given to Israel we read that the "double portion" was peculiarly the right of the eldest son. The father was to acknowledge the firstborn "by *giving him a double portion of all that he hath*: for he is the beginning of his strength; the right of the firstborn is his" (Deuteronomy 21:17).

In later scriptures we learn that when Elijah asked Elisha what he should do for him before he was taken away, Elisha replied, "*I pray thee, let a double portion of thy spirit be upon me.*" The R.V. margin says that he asked for the portion of the firstborn (2 Kings 2:9–10, mg.).

Elijah's reply was a strange one! He said that Elisha had asked a *hard thing,* but if he *saw* him as he was caught away, then his request would be fulfilled. Elisha *did* see Elijah as he was suddenly translated in a chariot of fire. Then "*he took hold of his own clothes and rent them in two pieces*" and took up the mantle that had fallen from Elijah as he passed out of sight into the unseen world. The mantle typified the poured-out Spirit which later fell upon the waiting disciples at Jerusalem—the gift of the ascended Lord to His church (Acts 2:33).

But why did Elijah say that Elisha had asked a "hard thing" when the portion of the firstborn was the *right* of the elder son?

The "double portion" of the fullness of the Spirit is a *birthright* for those who are born of God, but it is a "hard thing" to the flesh for the child of God to be truly broken enough for its reception.

Elisha took hold of his own clothes and tore them in two pieces! Even so must we be broken on every side before we can know in reality all the fullness that is typified by the portion of the firstborn son.

Truly Job's path to the double portion had been a "*hard thing.*" The breaking of the outward man had cost him many tears. His tenacity of faith in God (which is the spiritual meaning of Elisha's fixity of vision upon Elijah) had also been a "*hard thing.*" It was hard "against hope, to believe in hope," and surely harder still when stripped of "his own clothes" in the sense of being a broken man—stripped of all that had once given him authority and power—to take the place of intercession with God for others while still an outwardly *stricken* man.

The Son of God is expressly called "the Firstborn," for it is written: "When He bringeth in *the Firstborn* into the world He saith, *And let all the angels of God worship Him*" (Hebrews 1:6, mg.). But Christ was not only the Firstborn Son of God into *this* world, but *the Firstborn from the dead* into the *other* world.

The veil of His body was rent upon Calvary's cross as out of His pierced side there poured forth blood and water, a fountain opened for sin for all the world. He was carried into the tomb, arose from the dead, ascended into heaven and sat down at the right hand of the Majesty on high as "*the Firstborn of many brethren*" (Romans 8:29) who would be conformed to Him and like Him pass through death into life, through suffering into glory. For "*He is the Head of the body,* the church . . . *the Firstborn from the dead*" (Colossians 1:18) and, joined to Him, they are the "*church of the Firstborn who are enrolled in heaven*" (Hebrews 12:23).

The Father acknowledged the Son as the Firstborn by giving Him the anointing above His fellows. Yet *in* Him and *through* Him they too share in the double portion of their race—the race of "Firstborn" sons of God—they who will be partakers of the "first resurrection" (Revelation 20:6), "*heirs of God*, and *joint-heirs with Christ*, if so be that [they] suffer with Him that [they] may be also glorified together" (Romans 8:17, A.V.).

All this illumines the dealings of God with Job. He had known the power of the Spirit in his life, as we have seen in the description of his service, but through his fiery trial he has been led from faith to faith, and deepened, and prepared to receive "twice as much as he had before."

Again we see the wondrous harmony of the Scriptures and the unvarying message brought out in many and diverse ways in this wonderful book we call the Bible. With the immutable God, one day is as a thousand years and a thousand years as one day. To Him there is no time constraint, nor any change in His principles of dealing with His own. It is ever the same story, and one theme underlies the histories of all His people.

In *Job* we see the "hard thing" of the fiery trial, and then the double portion of his restoration—foreshadowing our resurrection life in union with the risen Lord.

In *Elisha* we see the "hard thing" of the fixity of vision upon the departing Elijah and the rent clothes, followed by receiving the falling mantle of the prophet of God.

In *Christ*—to whom all pointed and in whom all are again blessed—we see the "hard thing" of the death of Calvary, followed by the dispersal of the anointing Spirit and His own exaltation to the Father's throne.

Even so must it be for every member of His body. They must *choose* the "hard thing" of *fellowship with Him in His cross* if they are to be truly joined by Him as the Firstborn from the dead, share in the anointing He received above His fellows, and finally sit with Him in His Father's throne.

Unmistakably do we see again and again how truly

the Lord is the "First Cause" to His people.

The Blessing of the Lord

> "Then came there unto him . . . brethren . . . sisters
> . . . and all they that had been of his acquaintance."
> (42:11)

Job had said that the Lord had put his acquaintances far from him, and now the Lord *brings them back*! Brothers, sisters and acquaintances all gathered around Job when they heard that the Lord had spoken to him and had vindicated him to his friends.

Job's "house," too, was apparently restored, for he seems to have received his guests there and *"they did eat bread with him in his house"*—no longer afraid of partaking with an evildoer.

Moreover, Job was given the sympathy he had missed so sorely in his path of trial, and—being wiser, now that the sorrows were over—they "comforted him concerning *all the evil* that the *Lord* had brought upon him" (42:11). But how could they acknowledge that his sufferings had come to him from the hand of God and still *call them "evil"*? Job's troubles *were* "evil" in the sense that "*all chastening seemeth for the present to be not joyous but grievous,*" even though "*afterward* it yieldeth peaceable fruit unto them that have been exercised thereby, even the fruit of righteousness" (Hebrews 12:11).

It may be said that *no evil* can come from *God* as its source, and this is true; nevertheless, again and again we read that *the Lord* brought evil upon His people (Ezekiel 14:22; Amos 3:6; Isaiah 45:7). It is evident, therefore, that the Scripture means us to recognize *the hand of God above all* and *in all* that comes to His children; for "God worketh all things with them for *good,*" and resting in His will they do not see suffering to be "evil" any more.

Nevertheless, the Scripture does not hesitate to describe the sufferings of Job as *"evil"* because, in itself, apart from the purposes of God, suffering *is* an "evil"; and the God of Truth does not ask His children to call it anything else but *grievous* when they are *"put to grief in manifold trials,"* although they trust and praise Him *in them* and wait patiently for the "afterward."

Job's recent self-renunciation before God had also to be put to the test—in that the Lord chose the very ones who had forsaken him in his hour of need to now minister to him of their substance, for each one "gave him a piece of money, and every one a ring of gold" (42:11).

True, it was the custom in the East for presents to be offered when visiting a man of rank after a calamity. Nonetheless, it required self-effacement for Job to say, "The Lord took away, *and now He restores by the hands of those who failed me in my time of trial*—and yet—Blessed be the name of the Lord."

"So the Lord blessed the latter end of Job more than his beginning" (42:12). His wealth in flocks and herds was restored to him; sheep, camels, and oxen doubled in numbers,* and once again sons and daughters graced his home (42:13).

Obviously this time of restoration extended over months and years, yet the details of it are brief. The word-picture is painted with a few bold strokes. The very names of his daughters are revelatory of his restored prosperity. Every sentence of the narrative conveys, in oriental form, the fact of the unclouded favor of God.

As Job looked back upon his fiery trial, it must have been with chastened thankfulness to God, saying to himself: "He hath both spoken unto me and

---

* No doubt the round number is given for the exact number. This is often done in undoubtedly historical books—*Fausset.*

Himself hath done it. I shall go softly all my years. . . . Behold, it was for my peace that I had great bitterness" (Isaiah 38:15–17).

We may be sure, too, that Job walked before the Lord in after-days with a deepened godly awe and a keener sensitiveness to the sinfulness of sin. In the crucible he had learned to *know himself,* and he would go softly ever after in a chastened attitude of soul, bearing upon him in spirit the marks that Jacob bore in his body following his interview with God at Peniel.

By common consent the people called him "Job" (*Repentance**) for he was a "sign" to all, continually reminding them, by his very presence, that they must renounce themselves and turn to God.

One hundred and forty years did Job live after his fiery trial (42:16). He died "being old and full of days," having lived to see his sons' sons—according to the ideas of his time, a special mark of divine favor. He had passed through the fire, and in the fire had only lost that which would not abide the fire, while all worth keeping he kept unto life eternal.

We are told no more about the Adversary, but we know that he is still "going to and fro in the earth," "walking up and down in it," attacking with unceasing subtlety the servants of God—and yet again overreaching himself, in that they are brought *through* the fiery trial into a *deeper* and *richer* knowledge of God.

---

*Job's name comes from a Hebrew word specifying one who was "greatly tried," and is derived from an Aramaic word meaning *repentance*. It was common in old times to give a name from circumstances which occured at an advanced period of life—*Fausset.*

APPENDIX

RETROSPECTIVE NOTES

NOTE A
THOSE TO WHOM THE MESSAGE OF JOB APPLIES

It is important to remember that the special message of the book of Job is only applicable to those who have learned to walk in fellowship with God in integrity of heart, *exercising* themselves to maintain a conscience void of offence toward God and man, and unswerving in their fixity of purpose to abstain from evil up to the fullest extent of their light.

If we fail to recognize this we shall be thrown into hopeless confusion, for it cannot be said that those who are godless, or even those who merely *profess* to be Christians, with a name to live but actually being dead in trespasses and sins, are under the mighty hand of God in the special way in which the Lord dealt with Job.

NOTE B
THE PLACE OF SUFFERING IN THE SPIRITUAL LIFE

The book of Job reveals to us the place and purpose of suffering in the spiritual life. In the history of Job we are shown, subjectively, the stage of growth when suffering becomes *a necessary part of God's training* in conforming His children to the "pattern" Son, who is the Firstborn among many brethren.

In the history of Job the earlier stages of the Christian life are not depicted at all; the story *begins at the point where many place the goal.*

Job, so said Jehovah, was in His sight blameless (not faultless), true, godly and eschewing evil! What better description could we have of the life of victory over sin, of surrender to the will of God, and of obedience to the known commands of God? What better description of a life in the power of the Holy Spirit than that which fell from Job's own lips, recorded in chapter 29?

The story of Job's life therefore teaches us that the "life of God in the soul of man" must come to some *maturity of growth* before the child of God is ready for the lessons of the crucible, where he will learn to "endure unto chastening" and be dealt with as a son in whom the Father delighteth (Proverbs 3:12), and whom He scourgeth (Hebrews 12:6–10) that he may be a partaker of His holiness.

Job was an object lesson for the people of God throughout all time, therefore every aspect of trial was allowed to come upon him. With other of His children, the Lord will perhaps use but one of Job's many sorrows to bring them to the same place of blessing.

To some may come the loss of all earthly substance; to others the removal of loved ones to the heavenly home; and yet to others the stripping of strength and the lesson of helpless weakness. The All-wise Father knows each child of His love, the peculiar temperament and character, the particular danger and need; and so He lovingly adapts His training to the individual soul.

Some naturally love an active life, and need to be taught to lie still; others shrink from activity and would gladly live in quiet retreat. These latter He may choose to face the glare and pain of aggressive service, while the ones who love the bustle and noise are bidden, "Go, shut thyself within thy house." Others, again, are full of energy and strength, and only learn with bitter tears how to keep step with God, while slothful, easy-going souls are taught to find their *energy* in Him!

In any case, the Scriptures plainly teach us that, in many and varied ways, the ripest servants of God are *led through the same pathway of trial.* The "object lessons" are repeated, so that we may not fail to understand the ways of the Lord.

If we compare the language of David in Psalm 69 with chapter 30 of the book of Job, we see how both were led through the same deep waters in very different circumstances.

Again, if we compare Lamentations 3 with the same chapter in the book of Job, we find the words of Jeremiah and Job to be almost alike in the outpouring of grief in their hour of affliction.

Yet once more, we find a similar cry of the soul in the language of Jonah when in the belly of the "sea monster"—in this case specifically said by the Lord Himself to represent His own passage through Calvary and the grave to the right hand of the Majesty on high.

So that we may recognize the sovereign choice of God in dealing with His own, it is significant to note that *Elijah* was translated by a chariot of fire, not having seen death, while *Elisha,* upon whom his mantle fell, was taken with "a sickness whereof he died" (compare 2 Kings 13:14 and 2 Kings 2:12).

Joash, the king of Israel, wept over Elisha in his sickchamber and used the *very same words* that *Elisha* had used when *he saw Elijah taken away* before *his* eyes: "My father, my father, the chariots of Israel and the horsemen thereof!" Joash thus discerned in Elisha's deathbed the *same translation to glory* that Elisha saw in the chariot of fire that caught away Elijah!

Thus, in "precept upon precept, line upon line, here a little, there a little," does the Lord of Hosts, wonderful in counsel and excellent in wisdom, patiently teach His loved ones His varied ways of working in their lives.

"Whether we live, therefore, or die, we are the Lord's."

NOTE C
THE LORD'S OBJECT IN ACCEPTING THE CHALLENGE OF THE ADVERSARY

The scene in heaven conclusively shows that one object of Job's trial was to prove to the heavenly principalities and powers the *"manifold wisdom of God"* (Ephesians 3:10), for, as the heavenly hosts looked on at the tested servant of God upon earth, they saw the wisdom of God in His masterly way of changing the satanic attempt to ruin Job into a means of greater and richer blessing to his soul.

The Lord *proved to the angels* that His plan of bringing men through death to life was worthy of His infinite wisdom and His knowledge of the character of man. He proved, also, to the heavenly powers that He is able to obtain disinterested love and service from His servants on earth.

The Lord *proved to the devil* that Job did not serve Jehovah for all the blessings he had received from Him, and that all attacks upon the children of God only lead them closer to their Lord, so long as they trust the faithfulness of God and do not withdraw themselves from His hand.

The Lord *proved to Job* that the END of all His dealings with His children is for their eternal good, and that His character of love and pity is not changed when He places His servant in the crucible. Job himself acknowledged that Jehovah's dealings with him had been right, as in the searchlight of His presence he looked back upon his past, remembered his self-vindication, and loathed himself.

The Lord *proved to the friends* that a man could be justified before the Lord and walk with Him in integrity of heart, and that suffering is not invariably the result of transgression.

The Lord *proves to the children of God* through all the ages that they need the lessons of the crucible to make them know themselves, and, still more, a direct interview with Him before they truly can *renounce* themselves and know the abundant life in union with the risen Lord.

NOTE D
THE ADVERSARY AND HIS LIMIT

The glimpse into the heavenly court gives us not only knowledge of Jehovah's complete control over the Adversary but some knowledge of the devil's character and attitude towards the servants of God.

We are shown (and this is of vital importance to us today, over three thousand years since the story of Job was written) that the devil *sets his heart* upon every child of God who seeks to shun evil and to walk before the Lord with singleness of purpose and loyal integrity, and that he does not cease to use every subtle means to break their fellowship with God. Yet let us remember:

"I give unto them eternal life; and they shall never perish, and *no one shall snatch them out of My hand*," said the Lord Jesus to His disciples, adding, "My Father is greater than all; and no one is able to snatch them out of the Father's hand. I and the Father are one" (John 10:28–30).

The story of Job reveals the strength of the tie of life between the Lord and His children. The adversary is allowed to bring to bear upon it every possible test, yet it stands them all!

Property gone—but Job's treasures are in heaven! Children gone—but he had committed them to God and offered sacrifice for them, and they were safe in the Lord's keeping! Job himself, stricken and broken on every side, longs for death and cries to God to let him alone, but even in his anguish he refuses to part with the anchor of his soul! He persists that he is *in the hand of God*; and by his faith that he *was there,* he *abode* therein!

Let the redeemed take heed that they "keep [themselves] in the love of God" (see Jude 21 and John 15:9–10) and by faith abide under His mighty hand, so that He may exalt them in due time. Let them remember that the devil can touch them only so far as he is given permission by the Lord, but also only so far as *they give him permission* too!

The Lord may have permitted him to attack you on every side, but take heed that you give him *no further license than the Lord has allowed him* by listening to his whispered words that your God has forsaken you. "Hope thou in God and thou shalt yet praise Him, who is the health of thy countenance, and thy God."

NOTE E
THE HAND OF GOD

Cruden says that "hand," when referring to God, signifies (1) *His eternal purposes* and *executive power;* (2) *His corrections;* (3) *His sovereign disposal;* (4) *His providence,* etc., etc.

Job, in saying that the "hand of God" had touched him, meant simply that the sovereign will of God had decreed his afflictions.

Satan was obliged to acknowledge the sovereignty of God when he said to Jehovah, "*Put forth Thine hand now*, and touch all that he hath" and again, "*Put forth Thine hand now*, and touch his bone and his flesh.*"

Jehovah replied, "Behold, all that he hath is in thy power"—thus by His sovereign will permitting the attack of the enemy, while by His divine control He made it *actually* true that Job and his times were yet in *His hand.*

NOTE F
THE REFINING FIRE

In Ezekiel 22:17–22 the Lord tells Ezekiel that He will deal with Israel as men deal with precious metals. "As they gather silver and brass and iron and lead and tin into the midst of the furance, to blow the fire upon it, to melt it . . . as silver is melted in the midst of the furnace, so shall ye be melted in the midst thereof." For the house of Israel had become dross to the Lord, and the fire that was to melt them was the fire of His wrath in terrible judgments.

It may be said that a soul walking with God as Job did could not be subject to the same "fire" as Ezekiel described to Israel; but the Apostle Paul speaks of a "judging" of the children of God that is inevitable.

The "judgment" that is coming upon the world must begin with the house of God, that the children of the family of God be not "*condemned with the world*" (1 Peter 4:17, 1 Corinthians 11:32).

The "dross" in Israel and the dross in the character of the faithful servant of God are alike abhorrent to the Lord, and alike are to be dealt with by His fire.

It may also be said that the Lord *Himself is* the refiner's fire to His separated ones: "Our God is a consuming fire." But again it is written by Isaiah that He purges by "the *spirit of judgment,* and by the spirit of burning," so that both are true.

The All-wise Lord turns His hand upon His children to thoroughly purge away their dross (Isaiah 1:25) even while He Himself is like a refiner's fire in the midst of them, for it is written that He shall "*sit as a refiner* and purifier of silver, and He shall purify the sons of Levi [His separated ones] and purge them as gold and silver." Also, our glorified Lord, the Faithful Witness, speaks yet again as He did to the Laodicean church (typical of these last days), and counsels us to "buy" (or obtain from Him at all costs) the "*gold refined by fire*" that we may "become rich" and, clothed with "white garments"—white with the whiteheat of the furnace He has brought us through—be ready for His appearing.

"And some of them that be wise shall fall [or *be feeble,* as the word in the original means], to *refine* them [refers to the expulsion of dross by the smelting fire], and to *purify* [refers to the separation or removal of the dross already expelled] and to *make them white* [refers to the polishing and brightening of the metal after it has been freed from its impurity], even to the time of the end" (Daniel 11:35).*

NOTE G
JOB'S INTEGRITY

It may appear that Job was really "righteous in his own eyes," as he speaks so assuredly of his integrity before God; but we are given a glimpse into his actions at the beginning of his story which clearly explains his strong confidence.

---

* G.H. Pember in *Great Prophesies of the Century,* p. 417.

The writer to the Hebrews, referring to the sacrifices of Abel, declares plainly that the Old Testament sacrifices, offered in faith, *obtained from the Lord the witness that the offerer was "righteous"* (Hebrews 11:4) in the very same way as today the Holy Spirit bears witness to our conscience that "the righteousness of God, which is by faith of Jesus Christ, unto all and upon all them that believe," is ours as we draw nigh to God in faith—depending upon the "one perfect and sufficient sacrifice for the sins of the whole world," offered upon Calvary's cross when our High Priest Christ Jesus offered Himself to God.

Job's early rising to offer sacrifices for his children, in case they may have sinned, strikingly reveals his reliance upon sacrifice for clear fellowship with God. Job lived before the eye of God continuously, and feared sin so intensely that he was keenly alive to the least danger of disloyalty to God, even in his family. Therein lies for us today a deeply needed lesson if we would walk before God with the same integrity of heart.

Speaking in Paul's language, it may be said that Job *exercised* himself to have a "conscience void of offence," even as regarding his family and home. Only by this sensitive dealing with sin in practical life and entire dependence upon the effect of the sprinkled blood within the veil (see Hebrews 12:24; 1 Peter 1:2; 1 John 1:7), as cleansing our consciences every moment, can we walk with God and have the same witness borne to us by the Spirit of God. As it is written, "He that believeth on the Son of God hath the witness in Himself" (1 John 5:10, A.V.). "The Spirit Himself beareth witness with our spirit, that we are children of God" (Romans 8:16).

NOTE H
"The Wheel of Nature"—James 3:6

How little we children of God recognize the solemn truth that lies behind the statement of the Apostle James, when he says that the tongue is "set on fire by hell" so as to "*set in a blaze*" (Greek) the "*wheel of nature.*"

We may be desirous of renouncing the old life and yielding it to the cross but *frustrate* that desire at the very same time by—perhaps unconsciously—setting the wheel of nature in a blaze by our use of the tongue.

The Apostle James' use of the word "curse" in connection with this passage may have obscured its truth from us. We do *not* "curse," we say; and it is only the "cursing" of the tongue that is set on fire of hell. But the word simply means "*to wish evil to.*" The Lord's words in Matthew 5:22 may give us some light here. In dealing with the use of the tongue by the children of the kingdom, for whom He is setting forth the laws of the kingdom, Jesus says: "Whosoever shall *say* to his brother [another child of God], Raca"—an *expression of contempt*—"shall be in danger of the council [the council of holy ones in heaven who decreed the sentence upon Nebuchadnezzar]; and whosoever shall say, *Thou fool*"—an *expression of condemnation*—"shall be in danger of the hell of fire" (Matthew 5:22).

And He adds in another place, "*Every idle word that men shall speak*, they shall give account thereof in the day of judgment. For by thy words thou shalt be justified, and by thy words thou shalt be condemned" (Matthew 12:36–37).

The Lord therefore shows that words of *contempt*, words of *condemnation, idle* words, must all be absolutely put away by those who seek to walk as sons of the Father; and even *superfluity* of speech is said to be "of the evil one" (Matthew 5:37)!

Just so, the Lord recognized the evil one as the source of Peter's impulsive words to Him when he said, "Pity Thyself, Lord, this shall not be unto Thee." The Master said, "Get thee behind Me, Satan; thou mindest not the things of God, but the things of men" (Matthew 16:22–23, mg.).

Again the Lord said, "He that speaketh *from himself* seeketh his own glory" (John 7:18). Job had spoken from himself, and unknowingly sought his own glory (or credit) in his self-vindication. In his days of power, when his tongue had been so wondrously used by the Lord to counsel and bless others, did he think that in the crucible of trial that same tongue would sarcastically reply to misjudging friends, defend and vindicate his own character, and reproach his faithful Lord?

In this respect, the message of Job is a solemn one to God's children today. Contempt, sarcasm, condemnation, idle (unnecessary) words and *superfluity* of speech mark the speaking from ourselves, with the "wheel of nature" as the source.

With the tongue "bless we the Lord and Father; and therewith curse [or condemn and criticize] men which are made after the likeness of God: out of the same mouth cometh forth blessing and cursing. My brethren, these things ought not so to be (James 3:9–10). "Who is *wise*"—with the wisdom that is from above—"let him show . . . *meekness*," for the wisdom that is from above is pure, peaceable, gentle, full of mercy and good fruits.

NOTE I
THE MESSAGE OF JOB, AND ITS LIMIT IN GOSPEL DAYS

"Did Job know no more of 'trial' in his life on earth?" may be the question of some seeking heart.

But no direct answer to this is given in the sacred record, and we must recognize the *limit of the message of Job* to us who live in the fuller light of the gospel of Jesus Christ.

The old-time saints were "examples" for us, as Paul said, and all things happened to them "*by way of figure*," for "our admonition, upon whom the ends of the ages are come" (1 Corinthians 10:11).

The Scriptures not only contain the word of God to His people, but also a series, so to speak, of human photographs or picture-lessons of the outworking in experience of "the life of God in the soul of man."

In far back ages, from the majesty of the throne the Omniscient Lord looked down upon the little world of men and so controlled and guided each life surrendered to Him that it became, as it were, a canvas upon which He painted some *aspect* of His eternal truth, so as to teach in varied object lessons the finite mind of His creature man.

It has been truly said that "all saints" are needed for the apprehension of the breadth and length and height and depth of the love of Christ, which passeth (finite) knowledge.

Even so is the living Body of Christ knit together by that which *every joint supplieth,* according to the working in due measure of each several part.

In the same way, it may be said that the saints and prophets of the old dispensation minister to us, each one in his measure, some aspect of the truth of God—"to whom it was revealed, that *not unto themselves,* but unto [us] did they minister these things" (1 Peter 1:10–12).

In Job's case, the Spirit of God throws light only upon that part of his life which "happened unto [him] by way of example" for teaching us the special aspect of God's dealing with souls in trial.

The arrangement of the book bears the impress of

a Divine hand, guiding the record of the story for a Divine purpose.

The early stages of Job's life are passed over, and little is emphasized but his personal character at the beginning of his trial, and again very few words are considered sufficient to speak of a life that lasted one hundred and forty years after his trial was over. Instead, the light is focused upon a few brief months in his life history, when we are shown by "way of figure" the path of stripping and breaking down by which the soul is brought into a knowledge of God upon the throne of the universe, a vital fact never realized before.

The story closes with the account of the "abundance" of grace and cloudless fellowship with God which is the END—or purpose—of the Lord's dealings with every soul. But for *another aspect of the same abundant life,* promised to us in Christ Jesus our Lord, we must turn to the history of the Apostle Paul. In Job we are shown the abundance that follows the brokenness, but in Paul we behold the greater brokenness that is the further outcome of the abundance.

In brief, it may be said that after the soul has been broken on every side and brought into the abundant life typified by the "double" restored to Job, we are shown by Paul's history that it will be led, on the manward side, into still greater brokenness for the outpouring of life to others.

On the Godward side, the soul will be led from faith to faith, from strength to strength, from glory to glory; while on the earthward side, the outward man is "always delivered to death" and becomes increasingly a partaker of the afflictions of Christ for His Body's sake, the Church—until, in a very real sense, the language of the soul finds expression in the words of Paul the Apostle: "As *dying,* and behold, we live; as *chastened,* and not killed; as *sorrowful,* yet always rejoicing; as *poor,* yet making many rich; as *having nothing,* and yet possessing all things" (2 Corinthians 6:9–10). Like the Lord they serve, "*crucified* through weakness"—daily, even hourly weakness—yet living, in union with Him as the Risen One, by the power of God toward others for whom He died (2 Corinthians 13:4).

EXTRACTS FROM OTHER WRITERS

I. JOB AS A "FOREGLEAM" OF CHRIST

The idea of this great book is a solemn but blessed message for our time. It tells us pain may be rescued from its harsh associations and exalted into a high privilege. It may be only to test their loyalty and educate their trust that lofty spirits have to tread this winepress. Job was a greater character, and acted a loftier part in revelation and the history of religious thought and feeling, than he himself understood. For he lingered on the very borderland of the vicarious element of suffering, and was certainly groping after it. He was a type and shadow and foregleam of the coming Christ Himself. The suffering, upright man pointed the way to the suffering Sinless Man—the Man of Sorrows. The giant struggle to understand and interpret, for himself and us, his own cross, brought him into the dim and distant fellowship of Calvary and its great one Cross for the good of all. "The Crucifixion," Mozley has truly said, "is the one consummate act of injustice, to which all others are but distant approaches." And so all the suffering sons of God gather there, and, in the light of *that Cross*, they find the key that explains and justifies and glorifies their own. (*The Sacrament of Pain*—Rev. John Morgan)

II. ON THE NAME "EL-SHADDAI" IN JOB

It is in the Book of Job, and in the Revelation . . .

that we most often find the name "Almighty." . . . One can hardly understand the continual reference to "El-Shaddai" in [the Book of Job] without some apprehension of its distinctive lesson. The aim of the book is to show the sacrificial use of God's elect.

[All the friends] in their replies to Job—Eliphaz more often than the other two—refer to and dwell upon the name "*El-Shaddai.*" They seem to use it as a sort of proof that Job's troubles are a judgment for his sins, for "Shaddai," the "Pourer-forth," would [so they argue] surely bless the upright: and if, instead of blessing, he pours out judgments upon Job, then Job must be an evildoer.

The three friends agree that Job's sorrow must come from sin on his part. None of them have any idea of the sacrificial use of God's elect, or how by the sufferings of His saints God may be stilling the enemy and the avenger. Of these three friends God says that, with all their zeal to justify God, they "have not spoken of Me the thing that is right, as My servant Job hath." . . . Job is accepted and blessed in spite of all his self-assertion, and his perplexity, how God Almighty, being what He is, can allow him to suffer such varied agonies. But he understands at last.

Job, even as we, with all his uprightness, had to learn how self can live and please itself, not only in an irreligious and worldly life, but even in what looks like, and indeed is, real devotedness. Of this religious self he has to be stripped. And he is stripped by "El-Shaddai." The judgment of his flesh . . . brings him to the self-emptying and self-despair where the Lord, as the "Pourer-forth," can fill him out of His divine fullness. Job at once is freed and made a blessing. He prays for his friends and is accepted, and his "latter end is blessed more than his beginning." . . . After this Job lived a "hundred and forty years . . . and saw his sons, and his sons' sons, even four generations." Here was fruitfulness indeed. "El-Shaddai," whom he had invoked, though He had tried him, had indeed blessed him. (*The Names of God*—Jukes)

III. PAIN AS AN "EVIL"

Love cannot be explained, made manifest of what nature it is, the secret of happiness revealed, *except by an exhibition of the toil,* the abnegation, the *sacrifice,* that are in it. Seeking for happiness, craving for good, we grasp at pleasure and turn away from pain. God must teach us better, and to do so He shows us the root and basis of His own. Stripping off His infinitude and taking infirmity like ours, He bids us look and see! The only happiness He has, or can bestow, *bears martyrdom within it.*

It is sacrifice that binds us to God, and makes us most like Him: sacrifice that to us is sorrow, wanting life and love; but *to Him, supreme in both, is joy.*

And when we say pain is an evil, we can only rightly mean that *our feeling it to be pain* is an evil. That marks defect and want . . . shortcoming from our *privilege of joy.* From *pain* we may well seek and pray to be delivered; but by what deliverance? It may be banished in two ways—by taking away or by adding. Pain may be removed passively by the removal of that which is its cause, letting us relapse into mere repose, which may seem joy by contrast, or by the deadening of the sensibility, that shall banish alike pain and pleasure. But it may also be removed actively, positively; not by the absence of the cause nor by diminished feeling, but by a new and added power, which shall *turn it into joy*—a joy like God's. (*The Mystery of Pain*—James Hinton)

IV. COMPLETING THE SUFFERINGS

"I fill up that which is behind of the sufferings of
Christ."—Colossians 1:24

The suggestion is this—all ministry for the Master
must be possessed by the sacrificial spirit of the
Master. If Paul is to help in the redemption of Rome,
he must himself incarnate the death of Calvary. If he
is to be a minister of life, he must "die daily." Every
real lift implies a corresponding strain; and wherever
the crooked is made straight, "virtue" must go out of
the erect. The Spirit of Calvary is to be re-incarnate
in Ephesus and Athens and Rome, . . . the sacrificial
succession is to be maintained through the ages, and
we are to "fill up that which is behind of the sufferings of Christ."

Here, then, is a principle. The gospel of a broken
heart demands the ministry of bleeding hearts. As
soon as we cease to bleed we cease to bless. When
our sympathy loses its pangs we can no longer be the
servants of the Passion. I do not know how any
Christian service is to be fruitful if the servant is not
primarily baptized in the spirit of a suffering compassion. We can never *heal* the needs we do *not feel.*
Tearless hearts can never be the heralds of the Passion. We must bleed if we would be the ministers of
the saving blood. We must . . . by our own suffering
sympathies . . . "fill up that which is behind of the
sufferings of Christ."

Are we in the succession? (Rev. J. H. Jowett)

V. SUFFERING A SERVICE

The martyr service is but slumbering in all men who
are *responsive to the Crucifixion,* and is ready to obey
the call that summons it to action. It has been the

most active force in our world. The transcendent resistance it has offered has turned the scale in great epochs, and shaped new epochs, and changed the aspect of the world.

The suffering of the martyr is conspicuously a supreme service. It has been an energy which has pushed religions, causes, civilizations into victory. The *martyr affection keeps open the richest vein in our nature.* The profound canon of life is that "the amount of power an organism expends is the correlate or equivalent of the power that has been *taken into it* from without." Beyond all dispute, the martyr power expended in the service of the world is the equivalent of the *power of the Crucifixion received from the supernatural world* with which it is in correspondence. Never were communications from the glorified Christ received with such force of impact or answered with such force of response. The martyr gives the law to all service as the Crucifixion gives the law to him. (Rev. W. W. Peyton)

VI. Interior Suffering

There are as many grades of suffering among souls as grades of living among men. Suffering may be spiritual, mental, or physical, or all of these blended in different forms and degrees. When a soul abandons itself entirely to God, with a perfect intention to be conformed to Jesus, the Holy Spirit in a peculiar way establishes a disciplinary government over it, and takes charge of every form of suffering such a one has, whether outward or inward, and so saturates every incident, trial, and grief, with the providences and purposes of God as to make it work for good.

The Christ life is the life of the cross, but the way of the cross is the way of crucifixion, pain, mysterious

and unaccountable trials, delicate, keenest suffering. To use the word "cross" in any other sense is
only a poetical myth, suitable for trifling professors
but not for thoughtful companions of Jesus.

It does not matter whence spiritual suffering
comes; if the soul is truly yielded to God the Holy
Spirit will gather every thread of pain and weave it
through His loom into a gorgeous pattern of the life of
Christ.

I speak not of outward calamities and sufferings,
or of the sufferings of the rebellious and disobedient,
but of interior sufferings which belong essentially to
a spiritual life. Some of these sufferings are:

1. *The sense of utter weakness to accomplish the
great task of life.* We never see the true magnitude of
life until revealed by the Lord. Few people get even a
glimpse of the huge dimensions of their destiny, or
the solemn grandeur of existence. When the soul
discovers the real task of life, living for God looms up
like a vast mountain range, with such duties, privileges and lofty precipitous possibilities that it almost
takes our breath to think how we can climb those
giddy heights, walk calmly along those narrow ledges,
and stand on the apex at last, more than conqueror.
This produces not so much positive feeling of pain as
[it does] faintness, inward trembling, quivering awe,
before the majesty of God's will. But this quivering of
the heart, at times well nigh overwhelming, may be
so pervaded by the Holy Spirit as to make the soul
bow itself, like Samson taking hold on the pillars of
the heathen temple, in a supreme exploit for God.

2. *Heart loneliness*, by which the soul seems cut off
into a strange isolation from other souls. God intends to unite all holy souls in a divine unity and
fellowship, utterly inconceivable by our natural reason, but before that is accomplished He must take
each devoted soul in a private manner off to itself

and detach it from all things and creatures, because we have by nature thousands of little threads of instinctive, natural attachments, to localities, times, seasons, persons, plans, prospects, sweet memories, glittering day-dreams, or bright hopes. These threads must be snapped, the best natural affections circumcised, not that they are sinful, but the heart must be islanded away out in the ocean of God, that it may learn in solitude with Jesus how to love as He loves, and be attached to all things and beings as He is, in the order of God's will. Hence the soul going through this process of interior isolation must suffer pain.

3. *A holy, pathetic sorrow for sin,* without any sense of guilt. An abiding sorrow for sin is a holy suffering, needful for spiritual progress; it maintains in the believer the principle of perfect repentance, it deepens humility, it kindles the feelings of gratitude, it keeps the soul in touch with the precious blood of Jesus, it worships the attributes of God, it begets intercession for others, and thirsts for the perfect reign of God, when sin shall pass away from the earth.

This sorrow for past sins, for the horribleness of past inward sin, and for the awfulness of sin in the world, is a blameless, fruitful form of suffering, and, under the blessed touch of the Holy Spirit, is free from despair, despondency, or the least taint of bitterness.

4. *A sense of inward pressure.* A strange unaccountable burden, like a sad premonition, is the way of the cross. We pass through things in our spiritual feelings which lie entirely below the horizon of our understanding, and are like those storms in summer so far away that we see no cloud and hear no thunder, but only see little flashes of lightning on the distant horizon. Sometimes it seems as if our souls were seized with a giant hand, which seems to

squeeze us with a strange sadness or holy dread, and like frightened soldiers in the night we feel for our armor and rush into battle, as if suddenly charged upon by the enemy. Such feelings may result from the attacks of the enemy, but if the soul will keep recollected and give itself to deliberate prayer, such strange inward pressure will be followed by a quiet, blessed expansion.

5. *Bitter enmity from others.* Sometimes we get glimpses of the awful malice of Satan, and when his relentless hatred is clearly opened to our view it makes us cry like a little child at seeing a raging beast.

God mercifully hides from us the malice of Satan and evil spirits until He gets us close enough to Himself to endure the awful sight, and even then He allows us only faint glimpses that serve to bring us into fellowship with Jesus Christ.

But the Holy Spirit will at times let a true, humble soul feel the malice of its fellow creatures. David had presentiments of the bitterness and treachery of his fellows. Madame Guyon felt the bitterness and deceitfulness of strangers, and the Holy Spirit put her on her guard not to talk to them when she met them. There are times when we feel the intolerable hatred of people hundreds of miles away, whom we have never met, and others not seen for years, yet there come painful shootings through the heart, like arrows dipped in gall, and a painful sensation that they would crush us into the lowest earth if they could.

This is real inward suffering. There are facts and phenomena in the spiritual world not registered in man's narrow theology. The soul is greater than the body, and has many experiences not tabulated in books. This painful sense of being despised by our fellows, even by those professing great religion, yielded to God in humble loving prayer, will bring us great tenderness and charity.

6. *God seems to fight against the soul,* as if He took a rod and beat the inner spirit. Superficial Christians never have this experience; it is for those utterly abandoned to God. This is the suffering Job referred to when he said the Lord seemed to fight against him, and Eliphaz tells us that we are not to despise the chastening of the Almighty, when He maketh us sore (Job 5:17–18). In addition to all Joseph went through in Egypt, there came a time when the word of the Lord tried him (Psalm 105:19). This was the profoundest, most delicate suffering of all.

7. *God seems to deal with the soul as an enemy* until the heart feels bruised to its center, but this is followed with the most exquisite balm.

When we see the spiritual needs of mankind, the destitution of the poor, the darkness of the heathen, the distresses of those in prison and asylum, the neglect of religious care of children, and the unspeakable needs of the souls of men, and then see how little we can do, our hearts ache for the world. This is a holy form of suffering, one in which Jesus lived all His years, for a large part of His suffering was the limitation of the human nature He assumed.

8. *Inexpressible desire for God.* There are two divisions among religious people, those who serve God legally and those who serve God lovingly.

Even among the sanctified are two classes, the severe and the tender. The severe magnify the legal side of holiness and know but little of that longing desire for God that weeps and sighs for His ocean fullness. The tender-hearted saints magnify personal love for God, get bright visions of the person and character of God, long for Him so unutterably that the heart fairly breaks with sweet, seraphic pain to be lost in the shining abysses of His glorious being. This is a suffering angels might covet, yet a real suffering, that has the capability of absorbing all other suffering. To gaze at Jesus, to blessedly despise ourselves, and then to look away from self, with such burning thirst for Christ as to forget our unworthiness, and to pine for Him until the heart trembles with holy yearning—the breast expands, the lips quiver, the hot tears fall, the prayer is too great for words, and the soul almost faints to be taken up into the bosom of infinite love—this is the sweet suffering of the spouse of Christ when she says in the song of songs, "I am sick of love"—Song of Solomon 2:5. (G. D. Watson)

VII. THAT GOD MAY BE ALL IN ALL

Every advancing soul must come sooner or later to the place where it can trust God, the bare God, if I may be allowed the expression, simply and only because of what He is in Himself, and not because of His promises or His gifts. It must learn to have its joy in Him alone, and to rejoice in Him when all else in Heaven and earth shall seem to fail.

The only way in which this place can be reached, I believe, is by the soul being compelled to face in its own experience the loss of all things both inward and outward. I do not mean necessarily that all one's friends must die, or all one's money be lost; but I do mean that the soul must find itself, from either inward or outward causes, desolate, and bereft, and empty of all consolation. It must come to the end of everything that is not God; and must have nothing else left to rest on within or without.

It must wade through the slough, and fall off the precipice, and be swamped by the ocean, and at last find in the midst of them, and at the bottom of them, and behind them, the present, living, loving, omnipotent God!

A writer on the interior life says, in effect, that our spiritual pathway is divided into three regions, very different from one another and yet each one a necessary stage in the onward progress. First, there is the region of beginnings, which is a time full of sensible joys and delights, of fervent aspirations, of emotional experiences, and of many secret manifestations of God. Then comes a vast extent of wilderness, full of temptation, and trial, and conflict, of the lessening of sensible manifestations, of dryness, and of inward and outward darkness and distress. And then, finally, if this desert period is faithfully traversed, there comes on the further side of it a region of mountain heights of uninterrupted union and communion with God, of superhuman detachment from everything earthly, of *infinite contentment with the Divine will,* and of marvelous transformation into the image of Christ.

The soul's pathway is always through death to life. The caterpillar cannot in the nature of things become the butterfly in any other way than by dying to the one life in order to live in the other. And neither can we. Therefore, it may well be that this region of death and desolation must needs be passed through, if we would reach the calm mountain heights beyond. And when we know this, we can walk triumphantly through the darkest experience, sure that all is well, since God is God. (*The Christian's Secret of a Happy Life*—Hannah W. Smith)

This book was produced by the Christian Literature Crusade. We hope it has been helpful to you in living the Christian life. CLC is a literature mission with ministry in over 40 countries worldwide. If you would like to know more about us, or are interested in opportunities to serve with a faith mission, we invite you to write to:

Christian Literature Crusade
P.O. Box 1449
Fort Washington, PA 19034